T0318952

Cambridge Elements ≡

Elements in Public and Nonprofit Administration
edited by
Andrew Whitford
University of Georgia
Robert Christensen
Brigham Young University

HOW LOCAL GOVERNMENTS GOVERN CULTURE WAR CONFLICTS

Mark Chou
Australian Catholic University

Rachel Busbridge
Australian Catholic University

CAMBRIDGE
UNIVERSITY PRESS

University Printing House, Cambridge CB2 8BS, United Kingdom

One Liberty Plaza, 20th Floor, New York, NY 10006, USA

477 Williamstown Road, Port Melbourne, VIC 3207, Australia

314–321, 3rd Floor, Plot 3, Splendor Forum, Jasola District Centre,
New Delhi – 110025, India

79 Anson Road, #06–04/06, Singapore 079906

Cambridge University Press is part of the University of Cambridge.

It furthers the University's mission by disseminating knowledge in the pursuit of
education, learning, and research at the highest international levels of excellence.

www.cambridge.org
Information on this title: www.cambridge.org/9781108811682
DOI: 10.1017/9781108867825

First published 2020

A catalogue record for this publication is available from the British Library.

ISBN 978-1-108-81168-2 Paperback
ISSN 2515-4303 (online)
ISSN 2515-429X (print)

How Local Governments Govern Culture War Conflicts

Elements in Public and Nonprofit Administration

DOI: 10.1017/9781108867825
First published online: November 2020

Mark Chou
Australian Catholic University

Rachel Busbridge
Australian Catholic University

Author for correspondence: Mark Chou, Mark.Chou@acu.edu.au

Abstract: While local governments have traditionally been thought of as relatively powerless and unpolitical, this has been rapidly changing. Recent years have seen local governments jump headfirst into a range of so-called culture war conflicts like those concerning LGBTI rights, refugee protection, and climate change. Using the Australia Day and Columbus Day controversies as case studies, this Element rejuvenates research on how local governments respond to culture war conflicts, documenting new fronts in the culture wars as well as the changing face of local government. In doing so, this Element extends foundational research by advancing four new categories of responsiveness that scholars and practitioners can employ to better understand the varied roles local governments play in contentious culture war conflicts.

Keywords: local government, culture wars, urban public administration, Columbus Day, Australia Day

ISBNs: 9781108811682 (PB), 9781108867825 (OC)
ISSNs: 2515-4303 (online), 2515-429X (print)

Contents

1 Introduction

All politics is local, and the culture wars are no different. (De Leon)

Conflicts rooted in culture and morality – the so-called culture wars (Hunter, 1991) – are commonly seen as well beyond the remit of local governance. In dealing with the big and combustible questions of values and identity, culture war conflicts revolve around seemingly entrenched moral and ideological divisions concerning what is right and wrong (Fiorina et al., 2005; Bain, 2010). They are thus often inescapably national in scope. When Hunter (1991) first popularized the concept of "culture wars" in the early 1990s, he had in mind an all-encompassing conflict between the forces of orthodoxy and progressivism over the "meaning of America." For him, the conflict was fundamentally "a struggle to shape the identity of the nation as a whole" (Hunter, 1994, p. 4), which would cut across "class, religious, racial, ethnic, political, and sexual lines" (Thomson, 2010, p. 4). Likewise, when Patrick Buchanan famously declared a "cultural war" during his speech at the 1992 Republican Convention, what he was describing was a war for the very "soul of America" (Hartman, 2015, p. 1). Each time there is talk about culture war, then, it always seems to add up to the "national culture" (Marone, 2014, p. 135).

Local government has rarely been viewed as the tier of government where such struggles over values, culture, and identity play out. According to local government scholars, what makes local politics distinct from its national and even state counterparts is that it is rarely ideological. Oliver (2012, p. 7) writes in *Local Elections and the Politics of Small-Scale Democracy* that, "[w]hereas debates among 'liberal' and 'conservative' elites dominate national and state politics, most local governments are not amenable venues for contesting liberal, conservative, or any other ideological visions of social organization." Certainly, a political hierarchy has long existed in federal systems whereby the lower the level of government, the more limited and administrative politics was thought to be. If national and state governments have historically engaged in redistributive politics of the kind that draws citizens into contentious discussions about the state of their country or world, local governments have for the most part been relatively powerless – unpolitical even – acting merely as administrative arms of higher levels of government (Berman, 2003; Zimmerman, 2008; Katz and Nowak, 2017).

In *City Limits*, Peterson (1981, p. 4) declares that "[c]ity politics is limited politics." Unlike state and national entities, local governments primarily engage in what he calls developmental politics, administering initiatives concerning local land, labor, and capital (Peterson, 1981, p. 20). In practice, this has mostly restricted the lowest tier of government to the administration and resourcing of policing, housing, taxation, parks and recreation, schooling, medical services, municipal courts, public works, infrastructure and zoning, transportation, and local economic initiatives. Given this, and the desire to "attract industry to a community ... or to renew depressed areas within the city," Peterson (1981, p. 132) argues that "[c]onflict within the city tends to be minimal." Dictated instead by "homevoters" (Fischel, 2005), who can up and leave should they take issue with city politics, the local sphere is thus thought to operate largely outside the party political and ideological bubbles of federal and state politics, making large-scale disputes the exception rather than the norm.

These traditional administrative functions notwithstanding, recent years and decades have seen an increasing volume of local governments leap "to the forefront of ideological debates that used to be purely national in scope" (Kelleher Palus, 2010, p. 135). Divisive issues like abortion, same-sex marriage, feminism, school prayer, multiculturalism, school curricula, affordable housing, the environment, and, increasingly, national identity and history appear to have become a mainstay in the politics of many cities and municipalities, attracting ever more attention as objects of policy and administrative concern. Part of this is most certainly an outcome of local governments' increased capacity to solve community problems and manage the lifestyle changes of their citizens (Denters and Rose, 2005). But beyond that, urban politics scholars have also begun to appreciate that distinctive localized cultural and moral divisions, which separate individuals and groups within cities and regions, can produce conflict (Borer, 2006; Sharp, 2007).

In recognition of the fact that "a national culture is not an undifferentiated whole" (Rosdil, 2011, p. 3473), these scholars understand that cultural divisions and conflicts can take different shapes in different communities (Sharp, 1999a). Whereas sometimes the dynamics of city politics can act as a mitigating force in culture war conflicts, providing a counterforce to fiery national contestations, at other times they can inspire passionate conflict that far exceeds other spheres. In these instances and localities, questions about how one's home, suburb, or community is governed can potentially become explosive (Schleicher, 2007). Although Oliver claims that local governments are not ideological he acknowledges (Oliver, 2012, p. 8) that "[b]ecause citizens' local political involvement is predicated so highly on strong local attachments to their communities, a political firestorm can be triggered by what may seem to be the most trivial of causes."

While often less visceral and less frequently publicized than national skirmishes, when local actors, activists, and domains become embroiled in volatile cultural, ideological, and moral clashes, they can blur the distinctions between local, state, and federal (Brown et al., 2005). When this happens, ostensibly national debates turn into local issues that can incite culture war conflicts that fall neither within the conventional nor expanded purview of local government activity (Sharp, 1996; 1997; 1999a; 2007; Brown et al., 2005; Rosenthal, 2005; Craw, 2006; Sharp and Brown, 2012).

These challenges present local governments with significant governmental and administrative challenges. According to the political scientist Elaine Sharp (1996; 1997; 1999a; 2002; 2003; 2005; 2007) – whose research on local government and culture wars remains the most authoritative in the fields of urban politics and public administration – local governments do more than act as "first responders" in many cultural and moral conflicts. Their decisions on public resourcing and administration can sometimes inadvertently thrust them into the "eye of a [culture war] firestorm" (Sharp, 1996, p. 738).

1.1 Objective and Rationale

The objective of this Element is to advance understandings of how local governments govern culture war conflicts today. In the fields of urban politics and public administration, Sharp's work was not just pioneering, but remains the cornerstone scholarship on this topic. Sharp provides a foundational typology of local government responses to culture war controversies, which includes nine categories designating different levels of responsiveness and intentionality. She also offers a set of conceptual tools to explain why local governments may respond in one way or another. Yet, with her foundational research now over two decades old and ever more local governments wading into culture war disputes that are fundamentally different in nature, there is a need to synthesize and extend Sharp's insights in keeping with current developments.

Local politics has seen an injection of excitement in recent years, with prominent commentators pushing for a rethinking of politics that begins at the bottom of the federal hierarchy (Florida, 2017; Brooks, 2018). While not without their critics, these advocates have championed an "extreme localism" that sees communities addressing their own problems and building their own economies outside the confines of federal politics (Florida, 2017). This may be at odds with what cities can currently achieve (Liu, 2018), but it is nevertheless reflective of new ways of doing politics that sees local governments, together with a network of local public, private, and civic actors, lead on a range of controversial social, economic, and environmental issues. This emerging "new localism" (Katz and Nowak, 2017), we argue, is connected to two key developments that underscore the importance of rejuvenating and enlarging Sharp's foundational research on local governmental roles in culture war conflicts.

First, the face of local government has changed in important respects (Carr and Feiock, 2016). Not explicitly mentioned in the American Constitution, the limited powers that local governments do possess have traditionally fallen within the residual powers of their state legislatures (Grumm and Murphy, 1974; Writ, 1989; Gibbins, 2001). But the contours of this federal hierarchy are rapidly shifting. Decades in the making, this shift has less to do with the so-called home rule – a principle of American federalism which, in certain jurisdictions, enables local governments to exercise their delegated powers so long as they do not contravene state laws and constitutions (Barron, 2003; Dalmat, 2003; Russell and Bostrom, 2016; Hicks et al., 2018) – than a range of political developments and challenges that have resulted from increasing decentralization and globalization.

Decentralization has given local governments expanded authority over matters that may have once been the sole preserve of state and even federal governments (Somin, 2013; Levine Einstein and Kogan, 2016). Notwithstanding the federal colossus (Zavodnyik, 2011), localities have been actively asserting their independence at important intervals, becoming "laboratories of democracy" and political innovators in their own right (Shipan and Volden, 2006; Kincaid, 2017). Activists have not been oblivious to these shifts, nor to the comparative advantage they enjoy in smaller, local venues where their capacity to set or deny agendas can sometimes be amplified (Schattschneider, 1960). Similarly, while globalization may have eroded the sovereignty of the nation-state and undermined the capacity of national governments, it has at times had the opposite effect on cities. "Globalization not only creates a hyperconnected world," write Katz and Nowak (2017, p. 47), "it also opens up new means for expressing local identity and new possibilities for local development strategies." As the hubs and command centers of the global political economy, cities – and those who govern them – have thus found themselves occasionally in the driver's seat of political, economic, technological, and cultural change, whether they like it or not (Sassen, 2001).

Second, there are new fronts in the culture wars that require examination (Davis, 2018; Castle, 2019). It is clear that culture war conflicts have expanded into new terrains since Sharp first began documenting their local expressions in the 1990s and 2000s. The recent rise of populist politics has seemingly deepened ideological and cultural polarization, with culture war conflicts becoming more divisive and pervasive. For many scholars, to understand the current age of populism is to understand the important role that culture – specifically, cultural backlash – plays (Norris and Inglehart, 2019). Populists like President Donald Trump, some argue, have "pioneered a new politics of perpetual culture war" where, just about every policy issue is a wedge issue, not only traditional us-against-them social litmus tests like abortion, guns, feminism and affirmative action, or even just the president's pet issues of immigration and trade, which he has wielded as cultural cudgels to portray Americans as victims of foreign exploiters. These days, even climate change, infrastructure policy and other domestic issues normally associated with wonky panels at Washington think tanks have been repackaged into cultural-resentment fodder. (Grunwald, 2018)

While scholarly research on the influence of populism on the contours of culture wars is still playing catch-up with popular commentary, the political battle lines identified by Hunter appear to have hardened in ways that dramatize perceptions of social conflict and entrench partisan divides (Davis, 2018).

One of the consequences of this new populist politics is growing political gridlock and dysfunction at the federal level, which invests local governance with particular challenges and opportunities. America's deepening partisan divide now often stops the country's chief political leaders from reaching meaningful consensus or making difficult decisions for the nation as a whole. Against this backdrop, some commentators have called for a constitutional localism that would shift more political decisions and authority down the federal ladder (Hais et al., 2018). Others have used the situation to repeat their claims about federalism's virtues. But, according to the likes of Somin (2019a), it has been Trump who has done the most to make federalism great again. Indeed, as he points out, one unexpected consequence of Trump's presidency is that it has helped even progressives rediscover the merits of limiting federal power. As the legal fight surrounding so-called sanctuary cities – or local jurisdictions that have disregarded federal policy to deport undocumented immigrants – showed, there is growing support among progressives and conservatives alike for the view that states and localities can and sometimes should go their own ways (Somin, 2019b).

This Element seeks to critically evaluate, advance, and rejuvenate research on local government and culture wars in light of these developments. Following Sharp's own methodology of "conceptual clarification," we aim to ascertain whether her established typology of local government responses and explanations constitutes "a comprehensive listing of governmental roles in such controversies and whether the conceptualization of any of the roles requires refinement" (Sharp, 1999b, p. 7). In doing so, we find the need to extend her typology to include four additional categories of responsiveness that bring into clearer view the peculiarities of culture war politics and the different ways in which local governments and local government officials can be implicated in them. Specifically, our updated typology introduces an analytical dimension of ambiguity which acknowledges that local governments can respond to culture war controversies in subtle, often opaque ways that are neither self-evidently supportive nor unsupportive of status quo challengers; it also draws attention to new dynamics of local governance. The first new category we introduce is Unintentional Responsiveness, which recognizes that local governments can sometimes be swept up in a culture war issue without overtly intending to respond to it. Our second new category, Incremental Responsiveness, identifies the small and often piecemeal ways in which local governments can respond to a cultural or moral controversy without being overtly wedded to culture war conflict. The third new category is Nonresponsive Responsiveness, which recognizes that culture wars sometimes compel seemingly contradictory policymaking at the local level which boils down to the need to balance competing political claims. Finally, we introduce a fourth new category of Local Activism, which draws attention to new and emerging ways of doing politics at the local level that link local governments with a variety of nongovernmental actors, partners, and institutions.

Shifting dynamics at the federal level and increasingly incendiary cultural conflicts present unprecedented new challenges for local governments, particularly as they are called to govern unfamiliar issues that would have once been considered well outside of their remit. Now is thus a pertinent time to revisit and rethink the various ways local governments can respond to culture war clashes. Moreover, these developments invite a slight shift in focus, away from simply explaining "urban politics through culture" and instead seeking "to understand, interpret, and theorize the role of cultural conflict in producing politics in the city" (Sharp and Brown, 2012, p. 395).

1.2 Contribution, Case Studies, and Structure

In pursuing this line of inquiry, we contend that this rejuvenation should extend to local politics and culture wars beyond the American context. Presently, the literature in this realm is almost exclusively focused on the American experience. But the United States is not the only country where culture war conflicts have presented local governments with thorny policy dilemmas (Cochrane, 2004; Pruijt, 2013; Koch, 2017). Different as these contexts and debates may be, cross-national comparison can broaden empirical and theoretical understandings of cultural controversies and how they play out in different federal political systems. Indeed, in a rapidly globalizing world, many of the culture war issues that local governments must deal with are global in scope (i.e. climate change) or have parallels in other countries (i.e. same-sex marriage). As such, adding comparative scope allows scholars and practitioners to draw potentially instructive insights from other contexts dealing with similar struggles and issues. With a noted absence of "strong theory" to explain variation in local government roles in culture war conflicts (Sharp and Brown, 2012), a comparative perspective is also valuable in its own right.

Our study draws together American and Australian experiences, which share sufficient similarities to make their differences illuminating. Similar to the United States, Australian local governments sit at the bottom of the federal hierarchy (Brown, 2006) – although they are typically much weaker than their American counterparts, commanding less resources and with a more restricted mandate. Not recognized in the Commonwealth Constitution, local governments in Australia are largely dependent on higher governments for resourcing (Aulich and Pietsch, 2002; Grant and Drew, 2017). Local governments' share of own-purpose public expenditure is about 6 percent of total government spending in Australia compared to 24 percent in the United States (Brown, 2008, p. 439); among Organisation for Economic Co-operation and Development (OECD) nations, Australian local governments have the fourth lowest share of taxation (Bell, 2006). Australian local governments also do not oversee areas such as education and policing, which are the purview of state governments (Dunn et al., 2001; Gibbins, 2001). Instead, their roles are largely restricted to the administration of infrastructure and property services, health and community services, planning and development, water and sewerage, and selected cultural and recreation facilities. Finally, compared to America's 89,000 local governments, Australia only has 537.

Despite this, Australian local governments have not shied away from nationally contentious cultural and moral disputes. While the recent expansion from "services to property" to "services to people" is yet to shift dominant perceptions of local government as purely concerned with the "three Rs' of rates, roads, and rubbish" (Dollery et al., 2010), some Australian local government scholars believe that more local governments are now "place-shapers" (Dollery et al., 2008; Grant and Dollery, 2010). This conception sees local governments as champions of their areas and shapers of local identity and interests – both cultural and economic – in association with other governments, nongovernmental organizations, and private interests. Australian local governments can be understood as place-shapers to the extent that they engage, in limited ways, in "building and shaping local identity," "representing the community, including in discussions and debates with organisations and parts of government at local, region and national level," and "maintaining the cohesiveness of the community" (Dollery et al., 2008, p. 492). Together, these functions demonstrate the decidedly political and ideational roles Australian local governments play (Grant and Drew, 2017, p. 159). It is particularly against this backdrop that local governments have embroiled themselves in a variety of culture war issues, ranging from affordable housing, climate change, same-sex marriage, transgender rights, and the treatment of asylum seekers to employment (Gibbs, 2017; Slezak, 2017; Altmann et al., 2018). Australian local governments' comparative weakness only makes these interventions more intriguing.

Moreover, Australia's culture wars are closely aligned to those in the United States and sometimes follow closely in their footsteps (George and Huynh, 2009). If we are interested in how cultural conflict shapes local politics, as Sharp and Brown (2012) suggest, then this makes Australia a natural point of comparison with the United States. On both sides of the Pacific, as George (2009, p. 3) notes, culture wars thrive because "struggles for material survival have been largely overcome" making disputes over "post-material things" like culture, values, and identity more influential in shaping public debate. The histories and cultural developments of the two countries have intersected at various points in time as well. McKnight (2005, pp. 142–143) explains:

> Both are new nations in historical terms, which began as colonies of the British. Both are settled lands which were inhabited by societies of Indigenous peoples. Both developed industrially and politically without all the weight of custom and culture of tradition-bound societies in Europe. Both underwent a culture revolution in the 1960s and 1970s which questioned the role of women, rejected authority and established cultural identity as a central political concern.

Recent years, too, have seen culture war conflicts become more incendiary in Australia, with the middle ground seemingly out of reach on numerous cultural and moral issues as a more populist style of politics takes hold at the federal level (Davis, 2018). While populism in Australia has a distinct trajectory and manifests differently than in the United States (Moffitt, 2017), a notable point of coalescence between the two is that populist politics have breathed new life into nationalist causes. Müller (2019) writes that, among other things, the "populist art of governance is based on nationalism (often with racist overtones)." This has served to reanimate national culture, identity, and values as a significant culture war front in both countries.

1.2.1 Case Studies

In line with this, our Element explores two significant if underexplored comparative case studies: the respective American and Australian local government responses to culture war conflicts concerning Columbus Day and Australia Day. Local governments in the United States and Australia have played strikingly similar roles in these controversies, with many taking the lead – often to much public and political consternation – in changing or cancelling holiday celebrations in recognition of the harmful legacies of European colonization on indigenous peoples. Given that they address ostensibly national issues and federal public holidays, these two case studies can be particularly revealing of how cultural conflicts affect local and city politics. Along with the development whereby local and state politics have become nationalized in important ways (Schleicher, 2017; Hopkins, 2018), citizens now regularly conflate local and national politics and see their own backyards as a political battleground of national identity, culture, history, and values (Hartman, 2015; 2018; Somerville, 2015). How these cultural battles play out locally significantly impacts the tenor of similar debates nationally, thus offering insightful lessons into contemporary local politics and government.

As new culture war fronts (Liechty, 2013; Carey, 2018), the Columbus Day and Australia Day controversies symbolize the willingness of local governments to take decisive action on issues once considered outside their remit and, in some instances, their jurisdictions. They also represent the politicized role local government can play in culture war conflicts related to "big" issues such as national identity and values. Both in the United States and Australia, local government actions have generated heated debate, even drawing in Presidents and Prime Ministers; in Australia, for example, the Federal Government even used its powers to strip certain local governments of their rights to conduct citizenship ceremonies. Yet, unlike comparable issues like sanctuary cities, which have received significant scholarly, popular, and legal attention (Somin, 2019b), both the Columbus Day and Australian Day controversies remain decidedly understudied and undertheorized. In the United States, scholarship on the Columbus Day controversy has been primarily limited to indigenous studies and American cultural studies (Hitchmough, 2013; Lietchy, 2013), with most popular accounts by journalists and other commentators (Phillips, 2016; Murdock, 2018). In Australia, while scholars have highlighted the local level as a "rich site" for ideological disputes over nationalism, identity, and belonging (Dunn, 2005, p. 29), the roles of local government in the Australia Day debates have, with a few exceptions, by and large escaped academic attention (Chou and Busbridge, 2019). This is perhaps not surprising given the general lacuna in systematic research on the intersections of culture wars and local government in Australia. To date, scholarship on culture wars in Australia tends to focus on the federal and national level of politics (McKnight, 2005; George and Huynh, 2009), whereas scholarship on local government tends to overlook its roles and responsibilities in cultural conflicts (Ryan et al., 2015; Grant and Drew, 2017).

In exploring the culture war conflicts concerning Columbus Day and Australia Day, our Element applies Sharp's (2005) methodology in straddling the divide between large-N quantitative studies and single government case studies. Sharp's rationale for taking this methodological middle ground is that it offers scholars both a sufficient sample to compare and contrast cities to "yield evidence about the importance of various explanations for different local governmental stances" as well as the capacity to engage in "detailed examination of each one's recent handling" of the morality and culture war issue being studied (Sharp, 2005, p. 9). While large-N studies obviously come with the methodological advantage of generalizability, they typically preclude the capacity to delve deeply into the unique cultural, institutional, economic, and intergovernmental contexts and histories of a given city. Such an approach limits the "historical narratives" that "provide detailed evidence to support the classifications used to compare and contrast the cities' experience" with morality issues, as Sharp (2005, p. 9) argues. Our study suits this approach because our main objective is, first, to explore two exciting new fronts in the culture wars from a comparative perspective and, second, to revisit, test, and revise Sharp's typology. A large-N study might help provide a more systematic or definitive global picture of local government roles in these contemporary culture wars. However, it will not offer us the capacity to "fully and accurately depict" city narratives and developments in order to make an assessment of whether they fit – or do not fit – within Sharp's typology (Sharp, 2005, p. 22).

Specifically, we draw on a sample of ten strategically selected cities – five American and five Australian – whose local government responded to the controversies over Columbus Day and Australia Day in varying ways to enable meaningful comparison (Table 1).

Following Sharp, our city selection first applied a multivariate analysis of numerous cities which had prominent or interesting engagements with the Columbus Day and Australia Day culture war debate. The aim, like Sharp, was to ensure our cities had sufficient "variation on key explanatory variables and minimal correlation between explanatory variables" (Sharp, 2005, p. 22). However, given the comparative focus of our project, we had to deviate from a strict adherence to Sharp's methodology because many of the indicators she utilizes in her multivariate analysis to make sense of US cities (DeLeon and Naff, 2004) do not entirely translate to the Australian context. Sharp employs a multivariable assessment of cities' sociocultural type and economic development status in order to map and select her sample. Recognizing that measures of city culture and economic status differ in Australia, we examined a set of comparable indicators in selecting a diverse sample of cities to study. For economic development status, we took into account the city's population size and median income while for sociocultural type, we considered the percentage of the city's workforce in professional, scientific, technical, or educational

Table 1 Cases of local government action on Columbus Day/Australia Day

Issue	Case	Action
Columbus Day	Berkeley, California (1992)	The first local government to replace Columbus Day with Indigenous Peoples' Day
Columbus Day	Yakima, Washington (2016)	Council took less than one month to consider and vote on replacing Columbus Day with Indigenous Peoples' Day
Columbus Day	Los Angeles, California (2017)	The largest city to replace Columbus Day with Indigenous Peoples' Day to date
Columbus Day	Columbus, Ohio (2018)	The Mayor replaced Columbus Day with Veterans Day for budgetary reasons
Columbus Day	Seattle, Washington (2014)	Though the Council voted unanimously to replace Columbus Day with Indigenous Peoples' Day, much of the activism was led by one council member and local activist
Australia Day	Flinders Island, Tasmania (2013)	The first Council to abandon the community's January 26 celebrations in favor of a more inclusive, alternative celebration
Australia Day	Yarra, Victoria (2017)	The first Council to abandon its January 26 celebration and citizenship ceremony
Australia Day	Darebin, Victoria (2017)	The Council quickly followed Yarra's lead and abandoned its January 26 celebration and citizenship ceremony
Australia Day	Kingston, Victoria (2018)	The Council cancelled its customary January 26 event for budgetary reasons
Australia Day	Hobart, Tasmania (2017)	The Council decided to continue its January 26 celebration and citizenship ceremony while also formally joining the Change the Date campaign

industries, the percentage of the population with a bachelor's degree or higher, and the percentage of the population not adhering to a religion. The economic development status for each city is the average of standardized scores on the two indicators and the sociocultural type of each city is the average of the three indicators. Our chosen cities are presented in Figure 1, which illustrates each city's economic and sociocultural categorization.

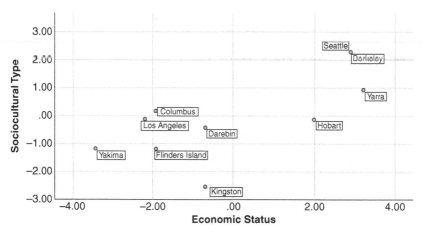

Figure 1 Case cities by economic status and sociocultural type

Another important difference is that Sharp distinguishes between chief executive type in her study cities. Given that there are no institutional differences between Australian local governments akin to the reformed/nonreformed distinction, we have not built these into our sample selection in a deliberate fashion, instead making note of the possible influence of such differences in the individual US city case studies. While type of government no doubt influences policymaking on culture war issues (Lineberry and Fowler, 1967; Taylor et al., 2014), Sharp's studies have found that the explanatory power of this distinction is weaker than that of other variables (see Section 2.2.3) so we hope this methodological inconsistency is forgiven.

The five American cities in our study are Berkeley, Yakima, Los Angeles, Columbus, and Seattle. Berkeley is among the most progressive and economically prosperous cities in our study. With a population of 121,363, the city's median income currently sits at $80,912. The city is often considered a home to political activism associated with progressive causes such as the civil rights movement, the free speech movement, and the hippie movement. The city's politics has been largely reflected in its City Council, which has been a site for progressive politics for numerous decades (Stein, 1986). Yakima, a city of 93,637 with a median income of $44,266, on the other hand, is the most conservative and economically depressed city in our sample. A center for agriculture, particularly hops production, Yakima is not a city many would associate with state-wide let alone national political causes. Yet what makes the city interesting is its proximity to the Yakama Indian Reservation and the Yakama Nation. Los Angeles, our third American city, is the largest city in our study by some measure, with a population of 3,979,576. As one of the country's most diverse cities, home to the country's entertainment industry as well as a number of Fortune 500 companies, Los Angeles, with a median income of $58,385, resists easy categorization. These factors therefore make it an interesting city to examine from a comparative perspective. Fourth, Columbus, a large city of 898,533 with a median income of $51,612, is slightly less economically depressed than Los Angeles and slightly more politically progressive. The city has a diverse economy, with key industries in education, government, banking, and defense. Finally, Seattle – the most progressive and economically prosperous city in our study – has a population of 753,675 and a median income of $85,562. Often considered one of America's most progressive cities, Seattle's economy is driven by Fortune 500 companies such as Amazon, Costco, and Starbucks as well as a range of other prominent tech and health companies.

Our five Australian cities are Flinders Island, Yarra, Darebin, Kingston, and Hobart. Flinders Island is the smallest city in our sample, with a population of only 906. With a median income of $53,092, the Island community's main industries are agriculture, forestry, and fishing as well as public administration and retail. Flinders Island is also notable because it is an island off an island (the state of Tasmania), which is itself off an island (mainland Australia). It is a remote rural community that rarely features in state-wide politics and almost never in national political debate. The city of Yarra is our most progressive and economically prosperous Australian city. It has a population of 86,657 and a median income of $101,816 and is situated in Melbourne's inner north. Yarra is a stronghold of the Australian Greens Party, one of the country's most politically progressive parties, and has long been a countercultural hub in Australia. Darebin, a city with a population of 146,719 and a median income of $73,996, lies just north of Yarra. Yet what makes Darebin different from Yarra is that it is currently undergoing gentrification. Thus, the city is more socially, culturally, and economically divided than Yarra – split between a younger progressive and older conservative demographic. Kingston is a middle suburban city with a population of 151,389 and a median income of $79,924. It is the most conservative city in our sample. Finally, our last city, Hobart, is among the more progressive and economically prosperous cities in our study. The capital of the state of Tasmania, Hobart has a population of 50,439 and a median income of $74,828. The city has in recent decades undergone a significant social and economic transformation that has shifted it from a conventional city to a postindustrial hub for the arts, culture, and tourism.

Having established sufficient variation across our sample cities through the multivariate analysis, we sought to establish a picture of how these cities have dealt with national holiday-related culture wars through a range of qualitative sources. These included local and national media coverage, relevant council motions and minutes, other policy and research documents, and speeches by or interviews with mayors and councillors. The media offers a rich repository of information relating to specific actors, decisions, and actions as well as the broader reactions of community members, political leaders, and other interested parties. Council documents, speeches, and interviews afford detailed information on key background factors, specific objectives or intentions, what (if any) consultation was undertaken, which councillor(s) spearheaded the action, and any divisions on the issue within council. For the Australian city case studies, we were able to additionally draw on original interviews that we conducted in 2018 and 2019 with key local councillors and mayors (Busbridge and Chou, 2020). Using the data gathered, we applied Sharp's framework to first categorize what these local governments did regarding Columbus Day and Australia Day and, second, explain why they might have acted in such a way. Following this, we identified and discussed the cases which either did not fit or did not fit neatly into one of Sharp's existing categories.

1.2.2 Section Outline

The Element is structured as follows. Section 2 elaborates on Sharp's work on city politics and culture wars, focusing on her nine categories of local government responses to culture war conflicts: *Evasion, Agenda Denial, Repression, Unintentional Instigation, Nonresponsiveness, Responsiveness, Hyperactive Responsiveness, Symbolic Responsiveness*, and *Entrepreneurial Instigation*. Section 3 explores the changing contours of culture wars in the era of populism and the potential implications for urban politics and local governance. Sections 4 and 5 examine American local government actions on Columbus Day and Australian local government actions on Australia Day, respectively. Using Sharp's framework, each section categorizes and explains why particular local governments responded in the way they did to the respective issues. Section 6 extends Sharp's typology by establishing four new local governmental responses to culture wars: *Unintentional Responsiveness, Incremental Responsiveness, Nonresponsive Responsiveness*, and *Local Activism*. We argue that due both to the relative weakness of local governments and the polarizing nature of culture wars, more subtle, incremental, and ambiguous forms of responsiveness are required to accommodate and account for how some local governments confront such conflicts. However, we also claim that the additional category of local activism is needed to encapsulate how some local governments and councillors perceive their increased role and capacity today.

A final word before we begin. While the primary objective of this Element is to fill a gap in scholarship, an equally important goal is to write a book that can be read and used by those working in local government to help them better govern the culture war conflicts they are facing. In this way, an Element provides an ideal format – given its short form and accessible nature – to inform mayors and other local government councillors and officials about the politics of culture wars and to offer them a practical manual that they can use to navigate cultural conflicts in their own jurisdictions.

2 Local Government and Culture Wars: Sharp's Typology of Responses

This section examines current American scholarship on local governance and culture wars, focusing on Sharp's framework for local government responses to culture war controversies. Although other researchers have studied the local dimensions of cultural and moral conflicts (Brown et al., 2005; Rosenthal, 2005; Sehorn, 2019), Sharp's extensive work has led the way in laying out a typology and set of explanations for scholars and practitioners to make sense of how and why local governments respond to culture war conflicts as they do. Even as we seek to update and extend research in this realm, Sharp's research remains foundational as it systematically identifies and categorizes the ways in which local governments can find themselves embroiled in prominent public "disputes grounded in moral concerns ... that are often passionate and strident" (Sharp, 1999b, pp. 3–4). Its importance is amplified by the fact that, outside the American context, there has been little systematic scholarship examining how local governments deal with culture war conflicts. Australian scholarship, in particular, lacks a systematic analytical framework with which to frame local governmental responses to controversies grounded in culture and morality.

For Sharp (1996; 1999a; 2002), the neglect of cultural conflict by many urban politics and local government scholars is not surprising. As she notes, such controversies challenge certain assumptions in mainstream urban political theory, particularly those concerning policymaking and problem solving. Importantly, because urban political theory is embedded in the political econ- omy tradition, which emphasizes material interests over values, "groups based on expressive and solidary values" are assumed less relevant to "policy forma- tion than ... materially based interest groups" at the local level (Salisbury, 1969, pp. 18–19). When conflict is considered, it is typically regarded as a question of "divisible benefits and assemble-able resources," with "compromise and coali- tion building" the primary goal of problem solving (Sharp, 1996, p. 742). But culture war conflicts, grounded as they are in values, are characterized precisely by their uncompromising nature: They are typically split down the middle, pertain to deeply held and emotive matters of belief and value, and are very often overlain by religious concerns (Sharp, 2002, p. 862). "The symbolic politics and morality issues that are at the heart of local culture wars," Sharp (1996, p. 742) writes, "are not readily treated as divisible benefits" nor do they lend themselves to easy compromise.

Even as they represent a departure from "politics as usual," cultural conflicts *are* an important aspect of local governance – and thus require serious scholarly attention (Sharp, 1996; 1999a; 2002). It is not just that local governments are faced with little choice but to adjudicate culture war conflicts when they break out in cities and communities (Schumaker, 1999, p. 193). As Hare and Poole (2014, p. 411) note, from "abortion, contraception, gay marriage, religious liberty, immigration, [to] gun control," local governments are regularly called to respond to "social/cultural battles" even if the lion's share of these issues is managed at the federal and state levels. It is also that these conflicts can have substantial consequences for local officials and the communities they serve. Outbreaks of culture war conflicts at the local level potentially produce a range of high costs, including those associated with maintaining social order, political blowback at local elections, and harms to city reputation and image, as well as the potential for property damage, injuries, and, in some instances, lives lost (Sharp, 1996, p. 743).

This is why Sharp developed her typology of local governmental responses to culture war controversies. As with other analytical tools in the social sciences, typologies draw distinctions between related cases and, through categorization of distinct types, provide new insights into the various dimensions of different phenomena (Collier, LaPorte and Seawright, 2012). Categorizing local government roles in culture wars as per Sharp's typology does not just cast light on those aspects of local politics eclipsed by traditional understandings of local governance. It also facilitates a more systematic picture of the options available to local governments when faced with conflicts rooted in questions of identity, culture, and morality (Sharp, 1997; 1999a).

2.1 How Local Governments Respond to Culture Wars

In some respects, creating a typology of local government responses to culture wars is challenging. Observers of local politics and culture in the United States are often struck by the country's incredible diversity. American local governments differ in terms of the level of professionalism, whether officials are elected or appointed, and the degree of autonomy from mayors and other officials (Sharp, 2005, p. 14). But there are not only fundamental differences in how local governments are formed and run, both within and across states: There is also a diverse array of local subcultures – again, both within and across cities – that influence how politics is done from one locality to the next. Institutional arrangements shape and constrain activism (Sharp, 1999b, p. 14), but local cultural norms and values additionally shape local governmental processes. For Reese and Rosenfeld (2012, p. 44), any account of policymaking needs to take the interaction of these factors into account: "Community values as well as decision-making styles and processes are tied to the power system, and these forces together comprise the local culture, which in turn shapes public policy." As episodes that are dynamic and often rapidly evolving, culture wars can invite multiple local government responses over the course of a controversy, as policymakers and other officials adapt to new mobilizations and developments.

Likewise, not all culture war conflicts are driven by the same dynamics or shaped by the same factors. Although there are commonalities, contemporary culture wars are ideologically complex. As Sharp (1996, p. 743) acknowledges, while such struggles would have been associated with Left activism in the 1960s, challenges to the status quo now come from both progressive and conservative camps. Take the case of abortion, which has remained a consistent point of social division in the United States. Since its 1973 federal decriminalization in *Roe v Wade,* localities have become central battlegrounds for pro-life and pro-choice movements. Reporting for *CityLab,* Holder (2019) notes that local lawmakers have taken advantage of zoning regulations in service of an antiabortion agenda, with "at least nine city governments making changes to their land use codes that either shutter clinics or restrict their operation" since 2013. Other cities have taken the opposing stance. After Ohio signed one of the country's most restrictive antiabortion legislations into law in 2019, Columbus City Council returned fire with a resolution that highlighted its "profound negative impacts on the health of women in Columbus" (Rosenberg, 2019). Furthermore, it may be possible to make a distinction between contentious and consensus culture wars: the former strongly divides public opinion while the latter has a clear majority on one side of the issue (Sharp, 2005, p. 192).

This diversity and complexity mean that clear analytical dimensions are essential to typology construction (Collier et al., 2012). Sharp draws on insights from social movement studies, political entrepreneurship, and agenda-setting theory in order to isolate two key dimensions that can be used to differentiate local governmental roles in culture war conflicts. For

Table 2 *A typology of local government roles in culture wars, adapted from*
Sharp (1996; 1999a)

Response	Not supportive of status quo challengers	Supportive of status quo challengers
First-order	Evasion	Responsiveness
	Agenda Denial*	Hyperactive Responsiveness
	Repression	Symbolic Responsiveness*
	Nonresponsiveness*	Entrepreneurial Instigation
Second-order	Unintentional Instigation	Unintentional Instigation

* denotes additional categories that were introduced in Sharp 1999a.

Sharp, these can be categorized in terms of whether local governments: (1) are supportive or unsupportive of challengers to the status quo, and (2) take a proactive or reactive stance in their handling of cultural controversies. They can be further delineated into first- and second-order responses: The former "are primarily based on the *intent* of local decision makers who take the action" whereas the latter hinge "upon the interactive effects of governmental actions and the actions of nongovernmental groups that are a party to the controversial issue," that is, the unintended consequences of governance decisions (Sharp, 1996, p. 753, emphasis added). With these key analyzing dimensions, Sharp identifies nine possible local governmental responses (Table 2), which we will now outline in more detail. In Table 2, we only summarize the key aspects of each response; the full account of each response, along with empirical illustrations, can be found in Sharp's (1999a; 2005) work.

2.1.1 Evasion

The key objective of Evasion is to preserve the political status quo by quarantining culture war conflicts through "low-key" and low-cost methods such as symbolically skirting, ignoring, deferring, confining, and even tolerating controversies so long as they remain discrete enough to go unnoticed by the broader public and media (Sharp, 1996, p. 747; 1999b, p. 25). According to Sharp (1999b, p. 5), the defining characteristic is to "defuse culture wars by delaying or deferring action on the demands of activists, making symbolic gestures to appease one side without activating the other, or otherwise diverting attention from what could be a heated or full-blown controversy." Evasion is thus the response of local governments that wish to deal with partisan politics with depoliticized governance, even when they may be sympathetic to particular causes. Sharp (1996; 1999a) notes that local governments can be expected to adopt evasion as a default response. This is in part because culture war conflicts can exact a costly toll on local residents and politicians, and in part because of the general reluctance – and incapacity in some cases – to legislate on morality issues.

2.1.2 Agenda Denial

Evasion can sometimes become a form of Agenda Denial (Cobb and Ross, 1997), a separate category of local government roles emerging from Sharp's (1999a) conceptual refinement. When Evasion becomes more than a one-off or ad hoc response to a cultural conflict, then local governments are denying activists the capacity to advance their political agenda. In this regard, claims against the status quo are prevented from ever being considered, thus denying them agenda status (Sharp, 1999a; 2002). However, Sharp (1999b) notes that if these efforts themselves become sustained and systematic, they then qualify as Repression. Agenda Denial might thus be understood as a response "in-between" Evasion and Repression.

2.1.3 Repression

Repression characterizes local governments that seek to do more than avoid culture war conflict: It is the position of governments that actively want to suppress activism altogether. As such, it is a more overtly political category than either Evasion or Agenda Denial. Drawing on Tarrow's (1994, p. 95) definition of Repression as raising the costs of organizing or mobilizing opinion, Sharp (2002, p. 864) argues that Repression can happen either through aggressive discouragement of protest actions – the "billy clubs" approach – or by making it "more risky, expensive, or difficult for morality issue activists to organize and send messages to potentially sympathetic publics"' Cities can also label certain causes and activists as "outsiders and inappropriate agitators," implicitly authorizing citizens to "intimidate those who would challenge the status quo" (Sharp, 1999b, p. 6). Repression can "impose substantial costs on local government" (Sharp, 1999c, p. 225; 1996, p. 748), including unwanted financial and legal repercussions or other spill-over effects, from unintended consequences for other local constituencies to undermining efforts to project a favorable city image. As such, Repression is more likely in "intense" cultural controversies, such as those involving hate groups (Sharp, 1996, pp. 747–748). Even though repressive actions typically face substantial legal constraints, Repression has become "one of the more common roles" played by local governments in the United States (Sharp 1999c, p. 229).

2.1.4 Nonresponsiveness

Nonresponsiveness, another category produced through Sharp's conceptual refinement, encapsulate situations when local governments refuse to make policy in accordance with culture war activists' demands (Sharp, 1999c, p. 231). Unlike Repression and Evasion, local governments will have debated and deliberated on the issue with the activists involved, making a "definitive and authoritative decision rather than [employing] tactics designed to avoid the controversy that might attend to such a decision" (Sharp, 1999c, p. 222). Examples of Nonresponsiveness might be when cities refuse to adopt gay rights ordinances or crack down on adult entertainment businesses (Sharp, 2002; 2003). An important criterion that is perhaps too implicit in Sharp's discussion is the requirement of procedural judiciousness and openness. For a response to qualify as Nonresponsiveness, the local government must have considered the issue using all the appropriate means and resources available to it. Put differently, purposely rushed or partial treatment of the culture war issue will not qualify as Nonresponsiveness.

2.1.5 Responsiveness

Responsiveness follows the same procedural requirement as Nonresponsiveness, with its main point of differentiation being a favorable response to status quo challengers. The key in both these categories of responsiveness is that local governments must exercise their typical scrutiny and be open to all interested parties in deliberations. Specifically, Sharp (1996) maintains that it is important that local governments hear from all sides of the issue and examine all available evidence. There must be no deviation from their typical procedures and conventions. Because the consequences of challenging the status quo will be borne by the community, local governments must therefore be procedurally and deliberatively prudent. They must also act collectively, meaning that Responsiveness requires consensus among a majority of council members (Sharp, 1999a).

2.1.6 Hyperactive Responsiveness

Local governments can also choose to throw their support fully behind an issue or activist, even when it is contentious or doing so will further exacerbate social tensions. If local governments respond to a culture war conflict in this way, Sharp argues, they are being hyperactive in their responsiveness. Hyperactive Responsiveness is premised on action that "(a) was relatively precipitous, (b) bypassed normal procedures, (c) disregarded obvious legal or constitutional issues, or (d) was a combination of these" (Sharp, 1996, p. 749). By adjudicating in favor of a status quo challenger in this manner, local governments therefore bypass the procedural and deliberative prudence that characterizes Nonresponsiveness and Responsiveness. For Sharp (1997, p. 271), "the short-circuiting of normal procedures" – a casualty of emotionally charged culture war politics or the by-product of a local government playing with fire – can impose potentially high risks and costs. Because of this, she claims that cases of Hyperactive Responsiveness are relatively rare (Sharp, 1999c, p. 231).

2.1.7 Symbolic Responsiveness

Sharp's (1999a) conceptual refinement identifies a fourth category of responsiveness. Symbolic Responsiveness is a way of responding to claimants without fully responding to their demands, primarily involving "rhetorical devices or gestures that do not really address the problem or substantively alter the authoritative allocation of values" (Sharp, 1999c, p. 221). Thus, it may be seen as straddling the divide between Evasion and Responsiveness, given that the status quo remains unchanged. But when it comes to culture war conflicts, even symbolic politics – such as painting rainbow colors to celebrate LGBTI communities – can be quite powerful because they afford symbolic legitimacy to marginal or unpopular struggles. For this reason, whereas Evasion skirts the issue, Symbolic Responsiveness brings more attention to it.

2.1.8 Entrepreneurial Instigation

Entrepreneurial Instigation is the most forceful in its support of status quo challengers. Here, local governments intentionally instigate or promote – rather than merely respond to – a culture war conflict on moral or principled grounds. When local governments become "political entrepreneurs" they "develop new and innovative policies and galvanize otherwise difficult-to-organize, dispersed citizens to support their policies" (Schneider and Teske, 1992, p. 741). In its purest, principled form, Entrepreneurial Instigation sees local governments "push morality issues onto the agenda even in the absence of overt pressure for it by constituency groups" (Sharp, 2002, p. 865). However, a government's decision to initiate divisive public policies can also be due to co-optation by some related social movement or ideological agenda (Sharp, 1996). This can provide the impetus for opportunistic officials to push their own agendas by riding on the coattails of prominent political movements and agendas. In these instances, local government entrepreneurs "exploit market opportunities and seek profits" for their own gains (Schneider and Teske, 1993, p. 318). Individual leaders accordingly play central roles in Entrepreneurial Instigation, either from deep-seated moral conviction or to reap political credit by standing on the "right side of a morality issue" (Sharp, 1999c, pp. 227–228).

2.1.9 Unintentional Instigation

In Sharp's typology, one response can be considered second-order, that is, lacking overt intention on the part of local governments to become involved in a cultural controversy. Unintentional Instigation designates those rare circumstances when local officials can inadvertently stoke political passions and produce unwanted consequences. While it can manifest in several ways, Unintentional Instigation typically stems from acts of Evasion or Repression gone wrong, which then spark local protest or activism. Repression, in particular, can result in Unintentional Instigation when it is sufficiently severe as to fan "the flames of resentment" among local activists (Sharp, 1999c, p. 231) or inadvertently frames a previously "nonissue in rights-oriented terms" (Sharp, 1996, p. 752). What is important here is that the local government has no concerted intention to trigger or exacerbate a culture war conflict. If anything, their intention is to quell the culture war skirmish or simply maintain the political status quo. As Sharp (1996, p. 753) notes, whether Unintentional Instigation supports or opposes status quo challengers depends largely on who is mobilized by the government action.

2.2 Why Local Governments Respond the Way They Do

Typologies are helpful in sorting and differentiating between cases, but they are only the first step in theory building. For Sharp, categorizing local government responses to culture war conflicts is a prerequisite for understanding *why* local governments respond in particular ways, that is, "under what circumstances should we expect to see local governments play one role rather than another" (Sharp, 1999b, p. 7). This is a question Sharp explores most thoroughly in her later work on morality politics (Sharp, 2002; 2005), where she seeks to assess the significance of *subcultural, economic, institutional,* and *intergovernmental* factors in shaping the responses of local governments to issues such as gambling, the sex industry, drugs, and gay rights. While her findings indicate that these explanations may not be equally relevant – depending on the morality issue – they each have significant explanatory value in making sense of local governmental responses (Sharp, 2005, p. 192). We outline each briefly in turn.

2.2.1 The Subcultural Explanation

Local cultural differences are one of the most important, if not decisive, factors shaping local government handling of contentious moral and cultural issues, according to Sharp. In this regard, her research can usefully be positioned as part of a larger project that underscores the importance of culture in subnational politics (Elazar, 1966; Rosdil, 1991; Lieske, 1993; Reese and Rosenfeld, 2012). This project has seen scholars draw distinctions between "liberal" and "conservative" cities as well as between "individualistic," "traditionalistic," and "moralistic" political (or civic) subcultures that hold divergent views on the role of government, relations between citizens and elites, and civic political participation (Elazar, 1966; Lieske, 1993; see also Sharp and Brown, 2012, p. 6). Sharp focuses on the values, affective commitments, and lifestyles of local social cultures, drawing upon the work of scholars such as Rosdil (1991) who highlight how urban cultures are produced by wider patterns of social change. Noting that "cultural change often sets the stage for political conflicts between the dominant culture and an insurgent subculture," Rosdil (1991, p. 82) suggests that postindustrial change in the United States has resulted in a cleavage between "progressive" and "traditional" subcultures. Progressive subcultures are the result of "new cultural practices" emerging from specific social trends, such as the diffusion of higher education, the changing social roles of women, the growth of nontraditional households, the growth of "human services employment," and the replacement of traditional religious values with secular ones (Rosdil, 1991, p. 81). Conventional subcultures, in contrast, are characterized by orthodox religious beliefs, traditional gender roles, lower levels of education, and employment in "goods-producing and extractive activities" (Rosdil, 1991, p. 81).

Following Rosdil, Sharp contends that unconventional postindustrial regimes are more likely to adopt progressive policies and welcome or encourage community activism than traditional communities; they are also more likely to make policy decisions based on cultural factors rather than simply on economic growth. Whether a local government is part of a postindustrial local community that exhibits "large, robust countercultures which challenge traditional social values" or an orthodox local community whose "overall social culture is much more traditional or conventional" will explain their roles in culture war conflict to a significant degree (Sharp, 2002, p. 870). Local governments in postindustrial communities will on average adopt a more responsive or entrepreneurial instigative stance in relation to status quo challengers than governments in orthodox local communities, which are more likely to adopt a repressive stance (Sharp, 2002; 2005). However, the *type* of morality issue is important in determining the salience of the subcultural explanation: It is only with "pure morality politics" – that is, where the issue is framed in terms of morals rather than material benefits or economic stakes – that we can expect to see such patterns of responsiveness (Sharp, 2005).

2.2.2 The Economic Explanation

In culture war controversies that have material interests, Sharp claims that local subculture will matter less than a pure economic explanation. "Material morality politics" involve issues such as the sex industry and gambling where there is a clash between morals and politics. These controversies, Sharp (2005, p. 197) suggests, are most likely to be guided by economic considerations when they have strong implications for the community's economic development or industries. The economic explanation can hold in other instances too. As local governments will be reluctant to pursue policies harmful to their finances, where culture war conflicts become bad for business, and damage the city's image, local governments will likely respond negatively to status quo challengers. Conversely, local governments may be more likely to respond positively when a culture war issue aids a positive city image and thereby encourages local investment. But Sharp adds an important caveat: "Although all cities confront pressures for economic development and have corresponding concerns about city image, these pressures and concerns are much more substantial in declining, economically distressed cities than in cities with secure economies" (Sharp, 2005, pp. 19–20). In other words, local governments in economically distressed cities will more likely factor economic considerations into account when they respond to culture war and moral conflicts than local governments in economically secure cities.

2.2.3 The Institutional Explanation

Sharp's research indicates that institutional differences may have only a limited role to play in explaining local government responses; in many morality issues, public officials often take positions on the basis of their own personal or moral convictions more so than the "usual political imperatives and constraints associated with their roles" (Sharp, 2005, p. 200). Nevertheless, public policy research on the distinctions between reformed and nonreformed city governments provide a useful rule of thumb as a means of institutional explanation (Sharp, 2002; 2005). First, the distinction between city managers in reformed cities vis-à-vis mayors in nonreformed cities matters to the extent that the former is a nonelected administrative professional who is protected from partisan politics, whereas the latter is a popularly elected leader who operates in a more politicized environment. Second, members of reformed city councils are elected at-large and members of nonreformed city councils are elected from single-member districts. While the former are likely to better represent citywide concerns, responsiveness to neighborhood needs is also reduced. Third, the use of nonpartisan ballots in reformed city elections reduces, in principle, party political electoral choices and outcomes compared to nonreformed cities.

Sharp (2002, p. 867) suggests that reformed city governments should be less responsive to, and more repressive of, status quo challengers because they "professionalize governance and minimize the accessibility of elected officials." On the other hand, nonreformed city governments should be more responsive to such types of activism. They should also foster increased opportunities for entrepreneurial instigation given "the greater ease in mobilizing followers" and "the powers available to a strong mayor to accomplish political innovations" – a mayor who is also likely to be more "attuned to political credit-claiming opportunities" (Sharp, 2002, p. 867). Finally, she posits that subcultural determinants will operate more overtly in nonreformed settings for the very same reasons (Sharp, 2005).

2.2.4 The Intergovernmental Explanation

Sharp's (1999a; 2005, p. 204) final explanation highlights the influence of other governments in constraining or enabling certain responses to culture war issues, though these dynamics will have most explanatory value in contexts of significant intergovernmental variation. Local governments, and the cities they represent, do not exist in isolation but instead are situated within *horizontal* relations with other local governments as well as *vertical* relations with state and federal governments. Horizontally, "cities learn from other cities that have been innovation leaders," especially when it comes to culture war issues such as "needle exchange or gay rights and [cities] adapt their efforts to control antiabortion protestors in the light of what has happened in other cities" (Sharp, 1999c, p. 236). While there is little strong theory on the influence of horizontal intergovernmental relations, Sharp expects that precedent and information-sharing networks will have some role to play in the policy decisions of local governments dealing with cultural controversies. Vertically, local governments can either cooperate with or counteract policies of higher-level governments, which, in turn, are able to shape local action through state and federal law and the allocation of resources like grants and information (Sharp, 2005, p. 20). Given that culture war activists "frequently turn to local governments for recourse" when "federal or state governments have been less than fully responsive to [their] demands" (Sharp, 1999c, pp. 234–235), local officials are most likely to take action when there are inconsistencies between local policy stances and those of higher levels of government. However, "the impact of local subculture on city officials would be most apparent where state law is consistent with the values of local subculture and least apparent where state law conflicts with local values" (Sharp, 2005, p. 21).

2.3 Conclusion

Two important takeaways emerge from Sharp's scholarship on local government and culture wars. First, while cultural controversies are a very real concern for local governance (at least in the United States), how these manifest and are dealt with by community and government leaders has been anything but uniform. Because cities are "not monolithic entities," it is "not necessarily possible or appropriate to identify a single role that local government plays in a culture war controversy," as Sharp (1999c, p. 232) writes. Scholars and analysts should accordingly view the responses laid out in Sharp's typology fluidly, not as distinct, complete, or mutually exclusive categories. Second, and related to this, the type of culture war conflict is critically important in understanding the actions and policy decisions of local governments and officials – as well as their unintended consequences. Just as local government responses are fluid and may change over time, cultural and moral controversies are likewise changeable and evolving as activists and issue entrepreneurs seek to frame them in ways that are to their advantage (Sharp, 2005, p. 192). There is thus an important need to elaborate further on the character and contours of culture war controversies, particularly as they play out at the local level. This is the task to which the Element now turns.

3 Conceptualizing Culture War Conflicts

This section sketches out the culture war concept, providing a more robust conceptualization of the character and dynamics of culture war clashes in local politics. While Sharp's work sits at the forefront of scholarship on local governance and culture wars, her research has tended to emphasize the local government side of the equation. The culture war concept – most developed in her earlier work, particularly in discussions of social regulatory policy (Tatalovich and Daynes, 1988) – is used primarily to highlight the intensity of social controversies as well as their irreducibility to economic and class conflicts (Sharp, 1996, pp. 739–740; 1999a). Her later work adopts a narrower emphasis on the "morality politics" (Meier, 1994) element of cultural conflict, with a specific focus on the legal and policy regulation of moral issues that have some religious component, such as abortion, legalized gambling, drug use, sex business, and gay rights (Sharp, 2005). Grounded as they are in questions of values, authority, and the nature of the good, moral society (Fonte, 2000), culture wars *are* profoundly intertwined with morality and religion, especially in the United States. However, this is just one dimension of culture war contestation. Other realms also extend to include diverse debates over immigration and race, the political choice of Left and Right, identity politics and the arts (Gitlin, 1995), as well as clashes over national culture, identity, and history as per our Columbus Day and Australia Day case studies. Moreover, the idea of culture war emerges out of certain social and political developments in Western liberal democracies that are only briefly theorized in Sharp's work (Leonard, 2012) and therefore not fully contextualized in relation to local conflicts.

If we are to update and extend Sharp's foundational research, it is not only imperative to develop our understanding of culture wars, but also to illuminate what has changed over time. "Almost any somewhat polarized conflict between disparate groups can be termed a 'culture war'," Bain (2010, p. x) writes. In the United States and Australia, national political discourse and the media have played important roles in crafting and fostering cultural polarization and contestation (George, 2009, p. 9), something that has become more prominent in the current populist era. Community conflicts are embedded in and framed by these wider dynamics, which do not just "ascribe value and meaning to culture and cultural values" (Leonard, 2012, p. 195) but also shape people's understandings of the local (Wills, 2015; Brookes, 2018). The Columbus Day and Australia Day culture wars bring this into clearer light. While the implications for local governance remain decidedly understudied, we contend that the current rise of populism signals new culture war fronts and different ways of imagining the local/national divide that local government administrators and scholars must familiarize themselves with (Antonisch, 2018).

3.1 Culture, Conflict, and Politics

The idea of "culture war" rests on a set of presumptions concerning the influence of culture in shaping perceptions of reality, the dynamics of social conflict, and the polarized nature of contemporary political struggle. These find most influential expression in Hunter's (1991) *Culture Wars: The Struggle to Define America*, a "ground-defining" text that reckoned with the existence of a post–Cold War "normative America" (Davis, 2018, p. 242). Drawing on the German *Kulturkampf* of the 1870s, which saw Chancellor Bismarck enact a variety of measures designed to defeat Catholicism as a political force, Hunter (1991) argued that contemporary America was in the midst of a similar struggle for cultural dominance. Rather than a conflict between religions, however, the new cultural conflicts happen *within* them; the defining feature is the fault line between progressives open to resymbolizing "historic faiths according to the prevailing assumptions of modern life" and conservatives committed to "an external, transcendent, and definable authority" (Hunter, 1991, p. 44–45). With historical roots in the countercultural revolutions of the 1960s and 1970s that witnessed the rise of feminism, multiculturalism, and libertarian social attitudes (McKnight, 2005), Hunter frames American cultural life and national identity as pulled between the impulse toward orthodoxy and the impulse toward progressivism, a dynamic of polarization that sees the middle ground eclipsed

(Thomson, 2010). For Hunter (1991, p. 42), cultural conflict is thus "political and social hostility rooted in different systems of moral understanding," with the ultimate end "the domination of one cultural and moral ethos over others."

Much of the scholarly debate over the culture war thesis has focused on the extent to which Hunter's depiction of cultural polarization is genuinely reflective of contemporary American society. While there continues to be ongoing empirical inquiry into the realities of social and partisan polarization in the United States (Davis, 2018, p. 243), broad trends indicate that there is more blurring than the culture war frame suggests. Thomson (2010, p. 1), for instance, asserts that "American public opinion is consistently more ambivalent and internally consistent than the image of culture war implies," with "most Americans occupy[ing] a position between the polar extremes." If culture is understood in terms of way of life, beliefs, and values, she continues, there is little evidence of incompatible cultures in the United States, at least not in the sense implied by the language of "war." For Thomson (2010, p. 17), Hunter overstates the internal uniformity and consistency of culture as "commanding truths ... deeply embedded in our consciousness and the habits of our lives" (Hunter, 1994, p. 200) when it should instead be understood as fluid, contested, and changing, as well as an object of political contestation itself.

Rather than viewing culture wars as the inevitable outcome of two, categorically opposed, systems of moral understanding, it is better to conceptualize them in terms of a political tendency to frame such differences in polarized terms. Certainly, as Hunter (1991, p. 43) himself acknowledges, "most Americans, despite their predispositions, would not embrace a particular moral vision wholly or uncritically"; the issue is how "*these differences are often intensified and aggravated by the way they are presented in public*" (Hunter 1991, p. 34, italics in original). Culture wars are thus about *public culture*: "the symbols and meanings that order the life of the community or region or nation as a whole" (Hunter 1991, p. 54). While political struggles over culture are not new, a heightened awareness that culture is political and politics is a struggle for cultural dominance is (Thomson, 2010, p. 2). Davis (2018, p. 243) argues that culture war discourse uses a "standardized set of simple binary constructs – orthodox versus progressive; conservative versus liberal ... – to caricature and reframe complex issues as a struggle between a virtuous 'we' and a demonic 'they'." It is less descriptive than rhetorical and polemical. Viewing culture wars this way has two important takeaways. First, culture wars are about framing all politics as moral politics. It is a political strategy to divide opponents and strike a chord with people; in the short term, they are about "shaping and mobilizing certain values in the community in order to win elections" (McKnight, 2005, p. 136). Second, culture wars frame public policy in terms of culture-based politics, that is, as a matter of moral values or a battle between Left and Right (Davis, 2014).

3.2 Culture Wars in the Age of Populism

While Hunter's thesis generated intense debate throughout much of the 1990s, the new millennium – and the 2008 global financial crisis in particular – saw the demise of culture war discourse both in the United States and in Australia (George, 2009; Hartman, 2015). Yet, in more recent years, a renewed interest in culture wars has emerged. The rise of Right-wing populism across many Western liberal democracies has seemingly confirmed Hunter's (1991, p. 307) warning about the threat of culture war polarization to the democratic ideal. With Trump's election in 2016, the United States has found itself in the eye of the populist storm. Comparatively, populism has had less electoral sway in Australia, but the country has nevertheless seen an upsurge in populist senti-ment since the 2016 federal election (Jackman, 2017). Like the United States, much of this sentiment has found expression in protectionist forms of national-ism with anti-immigration overtones, hostility toward minority groups, and a "jingoistic" approach to national identity based on the idea of cultural and geostrategic threats (Economou and Ghazarian, 2018).

There are clear points of convergence between populism and culture wars (McKnight, 2005). First, like culture wars, populism is less a specific ideology and more a political style or discourse that manufactures and overexaggerates social divisions for electoral gain (Tiffen, 2011; Moffitt, 2016; Jackman, 2017). Second, populism is often informed by similar dynamics as culture war con-flicts, including a backlash to progressive cultural change and social anxieties surrounding cultural or national identity (Norris and Inglehart, 2019). Finally, both culture wars and populism represent a departure from politics as usual, with the latter in particular characterized by antiestablishment values and a disenchantment with established structures of power (Koch, 2017).

But important points of departure arise too. Indeed, even though progressive/ orthodox distinctions *do* play a role in populist politics, these are less central than the presumed split between citizens and the political class or "the people" and "the elite" (Wills, 2015). In contrast to culture wars, populist polarization is framed not so much as a matter of morality than of popular will, with suspicion of the establishment complicating old partisan divides (Norris and Inglehart, 2019). Moreover, if culture war has found some of its most prominent articula-tions in the popular print media (George, 2009, p. 13), the current rise of populism cannot be disassociated from the "mediatization" of politics (Moffitt, 2016, p. 74). As Hay (2011, p. 659) claims, what is new about the rise of populism is "its articulation to and through a 'media revolution'." Social media and the explosion of new digital media formats have not only meant that the "spaces in which politics is conducted and discussed are increasingly porous" (Brookes, 2018, p. 1255); it has also signaled the hardening of opinions and the increasing palatability of extreme views and misinformation (Davis, 2018). The breakdown of trust in mainstream political institutions is amplified by this "post-truth" climate (Fraune and Knodt, 2018).

Whether culture wars have fueled the rise of populism, or vice versa, is not yet clear (Norris and Inglehart, 2019). But what is clear is that cultural conflict seems to have taken on an additional cast in the populist era, as politics becomes more fluid and interwoven with everyday social realities (Brookes, 2018). Post-truth politics, in particular, is believed to have established the conditions for increasing political polarization with the shift away from the center toward the extremes (Fraune and Knodt, 2018). Certainly, conflicts over national identity – always a staple of culture wars (Gitlin, 1995) – have only hardened into extremes with the rise of "nationalist populism" (Davis, 2018).

3.3 Local Politics and New Fronts in the Culture Wars

An important question remains: How do culture wars intersect with local politics and public administration? Although we have yet to fully theorize the local dynamics of culture war conflicts, scholars such as Rosenthal (2005) believe that place-based connections and the intimacy of everyday life in local communities "have the potential to mute the harsher side of elite polarization" seen in state and national culture wars as well as reveal "the centrality of political leadership styles in exacerbating or mitigating conflict and fostering community." As such, she suggests that there are three important attributes that characterize the local culture war front: "First, partisanship may be less of a factor at the local level. Second, many local communities lack the intense microscope of a super-critical media which add a dose of vitriol to our national politics. Third, local politics may have advantages in building social capital due to the benefit of strong place connections" (Rosenthal, 2005).

The extent to which these features have been transformed by the rise of populist politics remains hitherto underexplored in the local governance and urban politics literature. While we can only sketch them here, we contend there are two issues that merit consideration and might point us toward some of the ways in which local culture wars have changed in the contemporary era.

First, the issue agenda in culture wars has expanded into new fronts along with deepening political polarization of elites and institutions (Castle, 2019, p. 652). Of course, the content of culture wars is constantly evolving as older struggles are won or lost and new issues are highlighted by social movements, activists, politicians, and the media. However, it is important to note that American public attitudes to traditional cultural war flashpoints like abortion have become more ambivalent, with significant support for gay rights and same-sex marriage (Putnam and Campbell, 2010). In the context of continued progressive cultural change and a greater societal tolerance for diversity (Norris and Inglehart, 2019), Castle (2019, p. 651) notes that the New Christian Right has reoriented its politics toward a greater emphasis on religious liberty while also mobilizing on issues on which Americans hold comparatively more negative issues, such as transgender rights. It is furthermore the case that cities and municipalities are increasingly having to deal with potentially more explosive issues that extend well beyond the particular values and moral practices of local communities to more abstract communities like the nation and the world. Gun control, for instance, is a long-standing culture war issue in the United States (Melzer, 2009), but the increase in mass shootings in recent years has forced local officials into taking an immediate stand against media, public, and presidential attention, as happened in El Paso, Texas (Rupar, 2019). Likewise, the growing prominence of extremist, alt-right, and white nationalist groups have turned local cities into national battlegrounds – for example, the Unite the Right rallies held in Charlottesville, Virginia, in response to the removal of confederate monuments (Harbur, 2018). Climate change has also become a prominent culture war front that has played out in interesting ways at the local level, with post-truth politics and the politicization of climate change policy placing local governments in the position of having to arbitrate on what is effectively a global issue (Fraune and Knodt, 2018).

Second, populist politics has demanded a different conceptualization of the local. On the one hand, the populist claim that elites are disconnected from the needs and realities of "the people" buttresses the decentralization agenda in recognizing that power is too centralized and the citizenry are alienated from political processes. In this regard, populism and localism would appear to go hand in hand, with localism a new political ideal that seeks to shift power away from the national capitals toward city and regional leaders, local economic partnerships, local authorities, and citizens themselves (Wills, 2015, p. 189). While this may ostensibly be a positive development, it is important to recognize that the devolution doctrine remains most strongly supported by the Right, even if it is beginning to find advocates on the Left (Cochrane, 2004). On the other hand, the rise of Right-wing populism has occurred in an environment of economic instability, heightened inequality, and increasing xenophobic sentiment. Against this backdrop, cities have increasingly become sanctuaries of human rights, democracy, and cosmopolitanism (Smith, 2017) and may present more feasible political opportunity structures for progressive activists than the state or federal levels (Fetner, 2008). This is something well represented by the "sanctuary city" movement (Somin, 2019b) and the "human rights cities" initiative (Smith, 2017). As Smith (2017, p. 348) writes, while many movements mobilizing around "rights to the city" have conventionally been seen as outside the realm of "politics" typically defined, "in the aftermath of the election of Donald Trump, more are paying attention to these local initiatives, recognizing their potential to challenge the dangerous rhetoric and policies of the right." In this regard, the rise of Right-wing populism may be deepening the noted potential of the local as a site for civic leadership and collective problem solving, as well as societal norms of civility (Rosenthal, 2005).

3.4 Conclusion

In summary, this section has portrayed culture wars as the politics of cultural division and polarization; a rhetorical device or strategy employed to embed an us/them, Left/Right, orthodox/progressive dichotomy into public debates and policies. While the local sphere has traditionally been less susceptible to the worst of culture war polarization and politicization, we have argued that this state of affairs is now changing in the age of populism. Today, local politics is taking on a new cast as an important arena for cultural and moral contestation. This is something that local government administrators are increasingly forced to grapple with.

The Columbus Day and Australia Day case studies that this Element explores are in many ways a product of this new landscape. While neither issue is new, both have gained significant momentum in recent years. As cultural divisions grow more intense, cities and towns have been forced to take a stand. Significantly, on both issues it has been the lowest tier of government that has shown the greatest leadership. Through dealing with local issues such as parades, celebrations, and citizenship ceremonies, American and Australian local governments have made powerful contributions to debates over national culture, identity, and history, challenging conventional "geographies of democracy" (Wills, 2015). They are thus not only pertinent case studies with which to update Sharp's typology of local government actions, but also to demonstrate its continued relevance to contemporary local culture war conflicts. Analyzing local government actions on Columbus Day and Australia Day provides scholars and government officials with a much-needed overview of these politically important developments, with Sharp's framework an ideal tool with which to categorize and explain actions that may typically be thought outside the realm of local public administration and urban politics. In these situations, the act of categorizing and explaining can be particularly powerful – both in terms of aiding better understanding and of bestowing local government actions and actors with greater political legitimacy.

4 American Local Government Responses to Columbus Day

This section applies Sharp's typology to categorize and explain local government actions on Columbus Day/Indigenous Peoples' Day. Commemorating the 1492 landing of Italian explorer Christopher Columbus in the Americas, Columbus Day is one of the United States' most controversial federal holidays. Indeed, in the more than 80 years since it was proclaimed a day of national observance to celebrate the "discovery" of America, the October holiday has drawn widespread criticism concerning Columbus's place in American national identity, culture, and history, particularly "his brutal treatment of the continent's indigenous inhabitants" (Appelbaum, 2012). From the 1980s onward, Native American activists, including Colorado's American Indian Movement chapter, began protesting Columbus Day, deeming it neither a symbol of heroic discovery nor glorious achievement but instead the perpetuation of racist assumptions that indigenous peoples had no claim to their land and "should be grateful" for their colonization and dispossession (American Indian Movement, 1994). Taking issue with parades, holidays, and other events held on the day as a "celebration of genocide" (Appelbaum, 2012), Native American activists and their allies have been instrumental in calls to replace Columbus Day with more inclusive celebrations that go beyond acknowledging the cruel treatment and exploitation of non-white populations to "emphasize Native histories and Native people" in understandings "of what it means to be American" (Maynor-Lowery, 2019). In South Dakota, for instance, activists successfully persuaded the state to replace Columbus Day with Native American Day in 1989, and this has been marked as an official state holiday since 1990 (Doumar, 2018).

The movement to replace Columbus Day with Indigenous Peoples' Day has quickly gathered momentum – and strikingly it is America's lowest tier of government that has shown the greatest leadership. Though concerted calls to abandon the holiday appeared as early as 1977 at the United Nations' International Conference on Discrimination Against Indigenous Populations in the Americas, it was the decisions of South Dakota and subsequently the municipality of Berkeley, California, that became landmarks in the wider struggle (Liechty, 2013). Whereas by 2014 only a small handful of towns and cities across the United States had followed South Dakota and Berkeley's lead, by 2018 that number had jumped to more than seventy (Phillips, 2016; Murdock, 2018). As of 2019, at least 130 towns and cities – along with roughly

10 states and a number of colleges and universities – had decided against observing Columbus Day (Murphy, 2019).

Unsurprisingly, intense cultural divisions over Columbus's legacy show no sign of abating (Board, 2017). In one camp, "efforts to de-Columbus the US" (Doumar, 2018) have been celebrated as an affirmation of "the indigenous people who were in the North American continent long before Columbus" (Feeney, 2014). In the other camp, conservatives and members of the Italian-American community have criticized the movement as "political correctness run amok" and a blight on the virtues of Western civilization (Appelbaum, 2012; Murphy and Ortiz, 2019; Olsen, 2019). With the issue becoming increasingly polarized in the media (Thornton, 2017), the movement to replace Columbus Day has all the makings of a culture war that places American cities front and center.

While scholars have studied Columbus Day through the lens of nationalism and even as a culture war flashpoint (Hitchmough, 2013; Liecthy, 2013), there is little scholarship that has systematically analyzed the quite obvious and prominent roles played by local governments in this contentious issue. Given the 130 plus towns and cities that have acted on Columbus Day to date and the limited space of a short section, our approach will zoom in on and highlight a small sample of high-profile or controversial cases that illustrate the various ways in which local governments can respond to the Columbus Day issue. Consequently, we analyze the actions of Berkeley, Yakima, and Los Angeles – three very different cities that addressed the Columbus Day issue in different ways at different periods in time. Two of these cases are politically historic (Berkeley) and significant (Los Angeles), whereas one is based on unusual circumstances (Yakima), but all sparked controversy. Sharp's typology, we argue, aids in understanding the governmental rationale of actions that might typically be thought of as outside the realm of local public administration and additionally bestows greater political legitimacy on local government administration of culture war conflicts.

4.1 American Local Government Roles in the Columbus Day Controversy

Despite the wave of cities that have taken action in recent years, we must acknowledge that the vast majority of America's 89,000 local governments have either not entered this debate or decided against abandoning Columbus Day. This strongly supports Sharp's (1999a) claim that Evasion is the default response of local governments to cultural controversies. Even so, it is significant that several quite prominent cities have made the shift. Any overview of these cities will naturally preference those categories in Sharp's typology that are supportive of status quo challengers, but it is important to emphasize that we can expect a variety of explanatory factors to be at play. There has been an incredible amount of diversity in terms of how localities deal with Columbus Day. Not all have chosen to formally recognize Indigenous Peoples' Day. Some have elected to rename the day or celebrate both simultaneously (Murphy and Ortiz, 2019). Moreover, these localities are relatively diverse by way of demographics and local subculture. In addition to the "likely suspects" of progressive cities and those with significant native populations, Indigenous Peoples' Day is commemorated in several surprising localities as well (Maynor-Lowery, 2019). Brief as they are, our cases are intended to illustrate this diversity.

4.1.1 Berkeley, California

As the first local government to replace Columbus Day with Indigenous Peoples' Day, Berkeley's 1992 decision has served as a blueprint for cities now questioning whether their communities should celebrate the controversial holiday (Feeney, 2014). But even though Berkeley Council is today credited for its leadership on this issue, it was an activist local Indian coalition and a mayor keen to explore alternatives for the Quincentenary commemoration of Columbus's arrival in the Americas that sowed the seeds of change.

   The roots of Berkeley's decision originate in 1990, when John Curl, a local Native American resident, requested that Berkeley's mayor send him to the First Continental Conference on 500 Years of Indian Resistance in Ecuador to "gather information as to how the city should commemorate the Quincentenary" (Berkeley Indigenous Peoples Day Pow Wow, n. d.). Congress had already selected the Bay Area as the site of a national Jubilee that would feature replicas of Columbus's ships sailing in through the Golden Gate Bridge – and Berkeley's mayor, Loni Hancock, wanted to know her options. At the conference, representatives of 120 Indian nations passed a resolution calling for Columbus Day to be changed to a celebration of Native Americans in 1992, in recognition of Native resistance to European colonization (Phillips, 2016; Morgado, 2018). Inspired by this resolution, Curl, with informal support from Hancock, helped form a Bay Area Indian Alliance for counter-quincentenary planning in the fall of 1990. Among the Alliance's many initiatives was to organize a special task force called the Resistance 500 – comprised of committees in San Francisco, Oakland, Berkeley, and the South Bay – to "reaffirm October 12, 1992 as International Day of Solidarity with Indigenous Peoples" (Berkeley Indigenous Peoples Day Pow Wow, n. d.). The task force included Curl, Dennis Jennings, and Millie Ketcheshawno – the latter two would go on to become Berkeley's first and second Indigenous Peoples' Day coordinators (Curl, 2012; 2016).

Despite receiving behind-the-scenes mayoral backing, Curl, Jennings, and Ketcheshawno required City Council support. This came in late 1990 when Berkeley's Peace and Justice Commission and School Board requested that the task force be established as an official City body to develop activities that would "present an alternative view to the traditional Eurocentric presentations of Columbus Day"; this was approved by unanimous vote (Curl, 2016). According to Curl's (2016) record of events, that began a year-long process of the Berkeley Resistance 500 Task Force making presentations to different city commissions and lobbying public bodies on the concept of Indigenous Peoples' Day. The task force "finally reached the Berkeley City Council on October 22, 1991," and it voted unanimously in favour of making "Indigenous Peoples Day an official Berkeley holiday" (Curl, 2016). The Berkeley City Council Declaration encouraged local community organizations, schools, libraries, businesses, news media, and citizens to "reach out in solidarity with Indigenous peoples around the world and their struggles, including especially people indigenous to this local area and surrounding regions, to promote the health, education and welfare of all people, both immigrant and Indigenous" (Curl, 2016). Although the Declaration enjoyed broad support, it was not without criticism. Curl (2016) recalls that two of the City's conservative councillors were lobbied behind the scenes to reject the proposal, and they eventually brought counterproposals to celebrate the two holidays as a joint holiday. This quickly stalled due to lack of support. The Sons of Italy's Commission on Social Justice also criticized Berkeley's move, claiming, "it's kind of tough to rewrite history 500 years after it happens" (New York Times, 1992).

At first glance, Berkeley's action could be classified as Entrepreneurial Instigation given that it was the City's mayor who first sent Curl to the Continental Conference as her representative to gather information about how Berkeley should commemorate the Quincentenary. Moreover, although the Berkley task force did the heavy lifting, Mayor Hancock shepherded them through City bureaucracy, offering counsel and support, until they reached City Council. After the Council made its decision, she stood firm. Known for possessing an "incredibly strong sense of political morality" and "an inner toughness that wouldn't let her quit," even as a young councillor (Mundstock, 1985), Hancock told media that Berkeley's Indigenous Peoples' Day would provide "an accurate history" and no longer ignore "the brutal realities of the colonization of indigenous peoples" (TIME Magazine, 1992).

But the best categorization of Berkeley's action is Responsiveness, rather than Entrepreneurial Instigation. Responsiveness is characterized as a response supportive of challengers to the status quo that is nonetheless procedurally and deliberatively prudent. What is clear is that the origins of activism began well before Berkeley City Council, and even Mayor Hancock, became involved. In the Bay Area, the Bay Area Indian Alliance and Resistance 500 were the key instigators of change. It was the latter, in particular, that sponsored activities to resist "dominant culture activities," undermine support for the planned Quincentenary Jubilee, and work with local government to realize Indigenous Peoples' Day (Arnold, 1992). In this sense, Berkeley City Council merely responded to the Berkeley Resistance 500 Task Force's proposal (Tang, 2017). During deliberations counterproposals were considered both during and after the initial decision to abandon Columbus Day in favor of Indigenous Peoples' Day (Polignano, 2010). The whole process, which was a long time in the making, took over a year and canvassed all relevant city commissions and local public bodies.

To the extent that Berkeley was "a little bit in front [of other cities]," to quote Hancock (Feeney, 2014), this was due more to its responding to calls for change than to the fact that the City instigated activism. Sharp's explanations help us to make sense of this. Berkeley's reputation as a hub of counterculture is not only well recognized within the United States, but globally. In a surprisingly commonplace description, Ghasarian (1996, p. 48) writes, "that Berkeley was a place where anything goes exerted a powerful attraction for people who wanted to be where they could fearlessly experiment with different lifestyles." Rosdil's (2010, p. 118) research ranks Berkeley among the highest scoring cities on the progressive index, only marginally behind other "bastions of liberalism" such as neighboring San Francisco and Boston, Massachusetts. Curl, too, noted the Bay Area's progressive culture when explaining why residents did not want to "be the center of a national [Quincentenary] celebration of imperialism and colonialism and genocide" (Camhi, 2017).

These subcultural factors help explain why Berkeley exhibited both elements of Entrepreneurial Instigation and Responsiveness on the Columbus Day issue. However, the City's institutional arrangement as a reformed council-manager government helps explain why Berkeley opted for a responsiveness action. If Berkeley had a nonreformed government, it is probable that Mayor Hancock's entrepreneurism might have galvanized greater support – both among residents and other City Council members. As it was, her role was primarily to support the Berkeley task force as the main driving force of change. But the fact that the City Council nevertheless unanimously supported the Berkeley task force's proposal to recognize Indigenous Peoples' Day – something that a reformed government typically would not do – speaks to just how culturally progressive Berkeley was.

4.1.2 Yakima, Washington

Our second case, Yakima, is not a city that many outside Washington state would know very much about. It is not a particularly large city and, unlike Berkeley, it is not a counterculture hub that one would associate with progressive challenges to the status quo. And, perhaps most importantly, its 2016 decision to recognize Indigenous Peoples' Day could not be classified as significant by any typical standard. So, why analyze Yakima? The simple answer: speed.

Whereas Berkeley's decision emerged over an extended period of discussion, consultation, and deliberation, Yakima City Council took less than one month to consider and vote on the issue. It all began at an October 4, 2016 council meeting when David Powell, a Yakima resident and a Yakama Indian Nation archaeologist, "encouraged the City Council to change Columbus Day to Indigenous Peoples Day" during audience participation (Yakima City Council, 2016a). In response to Powell's request, which was not part of the meeting agenda, council member Holly Cousens promptly moved an unplanned motion, which Assistant Mayor Carmen Mendez seconded, to direct staff "to look into what other cities did to change Columbus Day to Indigenous Peoples Day with the intent for [Yakima] to do the same [the following year]" (Yakima City Council, 2016a).

Five council members supported Cousens's motion. Two members did not. Council member Bill Lover raised concerns that the issue was being rushed without sufficient opportunity for staff to review and the public to comment on the proposed change, while council member Maureen Adkison said she did not want to "lose a traditional day" and thought another day could be proposed to celebrate indigenous peoples (Bain, 2016). Responding to Lover and Adkison, council member Avina Gutierrez noted the personal importance of the issue and the need to pay tribute to the Yakama Nation (Bain, 2016). Her hope was that the move would create more opportunities for the City and the tribe to work together (Lyle, 2016).

Despite Lover's and Adkison's reservations, the City Council did not pause to review and further analyze the issue. Instead, they proceeded to draft a resolution to change Columbus Day into Indigenous Peoples' Day for the next council meeting on October 18. The resolution, which declared "the second Monday in October as Indigenous Peoples' Day" and encouraged "other cities and institutions to also recognize this new designation," committed the city to the "region's American Indian and Indigenous community, their long history, and their continuing contribution to contemporary society" (Yakima City Council, 2016b). However, for a document that was so clearly about the local indigenous community, it is significant that input from the Yakama Nation Tribal Council was sought only after the resolution had been drafted. Indeed, it was because the Yakama Tribe had not responded to the City Council by the October 18 council meeting deadline that the vote was ultimately postponed (Yakima City Council, 2016c) – but only until the following meeting. On November 1, the City Manager briefed Council on the resolution before it was officially adopted by a 5–2 vote, with Lover and Adkison voting against (Yakima City Council, 2016d).

From this account, it is clear that Yakima City Council's snap decision to replace Columbus Day with Indigenous Peoples' Day is very different from Berkeley's long journey. This contrast is precisely why Yakima offers a good comparative case. In comparison to the broad responsiveness of Berkeley, Yakima's decision is better captured by Sharp's (1996, p. 749) category of Hyperactive Responsiveness, which is premised on "relatively precipitous" action that bypasses normal procedures, for two reasons. First, the time that elapsed between Powell's request and the Council's vote to replace Columbus Day with Indigenous Peoples' Day was less than one month. In fact, had the Yakama Tribe responded to the Council's draft resolution – they had an eight-day window – the matter might have been resolved by the October 18 meeting, a mere fortnight later. Second, although the resolution was prepared by the City staff and submitted by the City Manager and City Attorney, council member Lover's reservation could have been heeded. Council member Cousens did instruct staff to look at what other cities had done. But this only formed the basis of the resolution, not as the premise of further feedback and debate. Here, the experiences of neighboring Seattle, Olympia, and Bellingham, which had all made similar decisions several years earlier, could have been especially instructive. The Seattle decision, in particular, generated widespread resistance from the city's Italian-American community (Beekman, 2014) while Olympia City Council's decision was a response to nearly forty residents who petitioned for the change (Hobbs, 2014).

So, why did Yakima rush headlong into this decision? Yakima is clearly not a Berkeley or Seattle, but an agricultural center known for hops production. Moreover, as a council-manager government, the City Council should have been less responsive to – even repressive of – status quo challenges. In the end, that it responded so favorably and swiftly perhaps relates to the intergovernmental context. Although Sharp's category of Hyperactive Responsiveness sometimes points to the bypassing of constitutional or legal requirements, this did not happen in Yakima. By the time Yakima made its decision, the initial trickle of cities recognizing Indigenous Peoples' Day had turned into a flood. In Washington and Oregon, cities like Seattle and Portland had made news headlines when they decided to abolish Columbus Day, paving the way for nearby cities to follow their lead. Not only is it likely that these earlier decisions influenced Yakima – here the concept of policy imitation might be a helpful explanatory tool to understand Yakima's action (Shipan and Volden, 2008); it is clear that the City wanted to become an influencer in its own right, encouraging through its resolution "other cities and institutions to also recognize this new designation." Finally, Yakima's decision would have been made easier – certainly less controversial – by the fact that Washington state does not formally recognize Columbus Day. A local government decision that does not contravene state government policies is always easier to reach and justify.

4.1.3 Los Angeles, California

Currently the largest American city to replace Columbus Day with Indigenous Peoples' Day, our third case study, Los Angeles, is significant not only because of its size and diversity. It is also significant because it represented a culture war in the truest sense, with two opposing constituencies – represented by two councilmen – defining the City's debate and ultimate decision.

The issue arose in November 2015 during the City's American Indian Heritage Month. Councilman Mitch O'Farrell, an Oklahoman of the Wyandotte Nation Tribe, proposed a motion calling Los Angeles to "honor the historic contributions of indigenous, aboriginal and native peoples by establishing the Indigenous Peoples Day as a legal City holiday" (Los Angeles City Council, 2015). O'Farrell's motion moved the City Council to instruct the City Administrative Officer and Human Relations Commission, with the assistance of the City's Native American Indian Commission, to report on the implications and cultural impact of replacing Columbus Day. In the subsequent months, the Council received numerous petitions from both Native American associations and members of the Italian-American community.

The City did its due diligence following O'Farrell's motion. Not only did it conduct extensive consultations with local Native American organizations, indigenous immigrant communities, the Italian-American community, stakeholders from the general public, and Native American studies specialists. As noted in the Housing and Community Investment Department and Human Relations Commission report from October 2016, the City also took seriously its responsibility to construct "a positive and affirming space for all residents," emphasizing Los Angeles as a "racially diverse metropolis" and home to one of America's largest native communities (Los Angeles Housing and Community Investment Department, 2016). Yet, while the report found broad support for

Indigenous Peoples' Day, it also revealed a marked division between Native Americans who felt "strongly that Indigenous Peoples Day should replace Columbus Day" and Italian-Americans who "strongly opposed replacing Columbus Day with Indigenous Peoples Day [identifying] Columbus as an important figure in their heritage" (Los Angeles Housing and Community Investment Department, 2016).

This schism resulted in a June 2017 letter to the City's Rules, Elections, Intergovernmental Relations, and Neighborhoods Committee, where Councilman Joe Buscaino, along with Councilmen Gil Cedillo, David Ryu, and Mitchell Englander (Buscaino et al., 2017), noted their support for "the creation of a separate Indigenous People's Day holiday," but argued that what Los Angeles needed was "the creation of a holiday celebrating Immigrant Heritage, in addition to an Indigenous People's Day holiday, because it recognizes the importance of unity and diversity." Buscaino, a first-generation Italian-American and active member of numerous Italian-American organizations, had expressed this view when O'Farrell first moved his motion in 2015, saying "I support the creation of Indigenous Peoples Day here in Los Angeles ... but not at the expense of another cultural heritage" (Loc, 2017). This letter formed the substance of a motion Buscaino moved at the August 2017 Council meeting, calling on Los Angeles to rename Columbus Day "Immigrant Heritage Day" and create an alternative Indigenous Peoples' Day to be held on August 9, the date set by the United Nations (Los Angeles City Council, 2017a).

The City Council rejected Buscaino's motion by 11–4. Mike Bonin, another Italian-American councilman, said he was pained to vote against Buscaino's motion, yet believed that Columbus Day undermined rather than celebrated his ancestors, who came to the United States to "build something and not to destroy something" (Zahniser, 2017). At this "fractious" meeting, which was attended by hundreds of activists (Rao, 2017), the Council also considered a separate motion, presented by Councilman Herb Wesson, moving that the City Attorney and Administrative Officer prepare an ordinance that would "remove all references to Columbus Day as an official City holiday" as per O'Farrell's initial motion and reports from various City committees (Los Angeles City Council, 2017b). Wesson's motion, effectively a return to and reemphasis of O'Farrell's, succeeded by a 14–1 vote, with Buscaino opposed (Los Angeles City Council, 2017c). Reiterating his opposition, Buscaino asked the Council not to "cure one offense with another," to which O'Farrell responded, saying, "we are not creating a racial conflict. We are ending one" (Rao, 2017). The decision was met with both cheers and jeers by the many Native American and Italian-American activists in attendance. After the vote, these activists took to the

Council forecourt, where O'Farrell and Buscaino joined them. Among the many speeches, O'Farrell quoted Lakota activist Bill Means in calling Columbus a "mascot of American colonialism in the Western Hemisphere," while Buscaino declared that "with or without Columbus, Italians will continue to celebrate their sacrifices and contributions to this great country and this great city" (Schmidt, 2017).

Los Angeles' decision demonstrates that even amid sharp ideological divisions, categorization of the local government action can nevertheless be straightforward. After all, Los Angeles' action is a clear instance of principled Entrepreneurial Instigation. O'Farrell's 2015 motion was inspired, in his words, by "the folly of celebrating a man who brought nothing but catastrophe for native peoples when he first arrived in the new world" (McReynolds, 2015). It was the hope of rectifying this historical wrong that motivated his motion. The series of debates and deliberations that he initiated did not appear to be the direct result of "overt pressure" by advocates pushing for Indigenous Peoples' Day, to use Sharp's terminology, though by late 2015 the indirect influence of other cities abandoning Columbus Day would have been clear. In particular, Anadarko had become the first Oklahoman city to recognize Indigenous Peoples' Day only two months before O'Farrell proposed his motion (Jan, 2015). As an Oklahoman native, this would surely have influenced his thinking (Norwood, 2016). Without O'Farrell, Los Angeles might not have addressed the issue when it did. It is a testament to O'Farrell that even today when people talk of Indigenous Peoples' Day in Los Angeles his name is never far away.

Sharp's explanations help us understand why O'Farrell's entrepreneurism – a rare local government response to culture war issues – succeeded in this instance. Although America's second largest city is too big and diverse to pigeonhole, modern Los Angeles and, in particular, O'Farrell's district which comprises neighborhoods such as Echo Park, Hollywood, and Silver Lake, is home to one of "the largest countercultures in the world, along with a variety of other radical movements" (McBride, 2010, p. 307). With New Left ideals of counterculture having "achieved the status of conventional wisdom among post-1960s liberals" (McBride, 2010, p. 317), there is no doubt that Los Angeles' broadly progressive ethos played a role in the willingness to challenge the status quo. Of course, this is not to say that all Los Angeles residents are progressive. That this case was so defined by O'Farrell's and Buscaino's opposition to each other also speaks, to some extent, to the ideological divisions evident in this hugely diverse city. It is furthermore pertinent to note that Los Angeles, a charter city with significant political and governmental autonomy, has a mayor-council government. Under these conditions, as Sharp contends, city administration tends to be more politicized and predisposed to entrepreneurism. Although leadership on Indigenous Peoples' Day did not come from the mayor, Los Angeles' government allowed for O'Farrell and Buscaino to lead the charge. In doing so, it also exposed itself to activists' demands on both sides of the debate.

Economic considerations offer an explanation as to why Los Angeles City Council was so quick to shut down Buscaino's counterproposal. The City's report had shown that while there was broad support for Indigenous Peoples' Day in Los Angeles, there was little consensus about how the holiday should be implemented. In view of this, Buscaino's counterproposal should have had broad appeal given that it presented a compromise. Finances are a powerful reason why it was unanimously rejected. Creating a new holiday to celebrate indigenous peoples, the report noted, would cost the City an estimated $2 million in overtime or $9.2 million in "soft" costs from reduced productivity, "a fiscal challenge, given all other budget priorities facing the city" (Los Angeles Housing and Community Investment Department, 2016).

There may have also been intergovernmental considerations at play in Los Angeles' decision, with the report observing that the move to replace Columbus Day with Indigenous Peoples' Day had already become something of a national trend by 2016. Also important was the fact that the City Council's vote occurred during a time of growing national discussion about the cultural legacies commemorated by some of the country's holidays and historical monuments (Zahniser, 2017). But ultimately, what may have helped the City Council side with O'Farrell's proposal over Buscaino's was former California Governor Arnold Schwarzenegger's 2009 decision to abandon Columbus Day as a state holiday for budgetary reasons (Schmidt, 2017). As with Yakima and Washington state, a local government decision that does not contradict state policies is easier to defend.

4.2 Conclusion

This section has highlighted two important points about local government action with respect to Columbus Day. First, outward similarities between how cities respond can hide important differences. Despite only analyzing three cities that ostensibly acted in similar ways, we have demonstrated that replacing Columbus Day with Indigenous Peoples' Day is where the similarities end (Table 3). If a more nuanced understanding and mature debate about how local governments are responding to the push to celebrate Indigenous Peoples' Day is what is needed, then these differences – and their varying motivations – can be illuminating.

Table 3 Local government action on Columbus Day

Case	Action
Berkeley, California (1992)	Responsiveness
Yakima, Washington (2016)	Hyperactive Responsiveness
Los Angeles, California (2017)	Entrepreneurial Instigation

Second, categorizing how and why cities act the way they do on this issue offers cities now grappling with this same decision a more accurate guide that they can consult to ensure they draw from a precedent that actually reflects their own context and conditions. Simply noting the flood of cities abandoning Columbus Day for Indigenous Peoples' Day offers only a rallying cry. A more sober discussion about whether a city should join the growing list of cities that have taken the step to replace Columbus Day may therefore benefit from the precision and explanations that Sharp's framework offers.

5 Australian Local Government Responses to Australia Day

This section applies Sharp's typology to understand the roles and responses of three high-profile or instructive local government actions on the Australia Day culture war. There are striking parallels between the Columbus Day and Australia Day controversies. Celebrated annually on January 26, few yearly events on the Australian national calendar are more divisive than the Australia Day national holiday (Carey, 2018). While it has only been celebrated as a public holiday in all states and territories since 1994, the date – which marks the 1788 arrival of British ships to what is now Sydney – has long been troubling for Australia's indigenous peoples, many of whom see January 26 as a "day of mourning" representing "Whiteman's seizure of our country" (Kwan, 2007, p. 10). With each passing year, political debate about Australia Day only becomes more contentious, with firm lines dividing those who see it as a symbol of invasion and colonization and those who believe it a legitimate day to celebrate Australia's national achievements. The main point of contention is not so much about whether Australia Day should be replaced with something else, but the actual day on which it is celebrated. On the one hand, January 26 is now the focus of large and growing annual "Invasion Day" and "Survival Day" protests in major towns and cities across Australia, which entail an array of alternative events, including indigenous-led marches and ceremonies that commemorate colonial frontier killings and massacres of Aboriginal peoples. On the other hand, there is a popular move-ment to "Change the Date," which advocates the importance of holding

Australia's national holiday on a day that is inclusive of indigenous and nonindigenous peoples alike.

Local governments have not just been prominent in these debates; they have been central protagonists igniting culture war divisions over Australia Day (Chou and Busbridge, 2019). While only nine local councils have thus far taken the step to officially abandon Australia Day celebrations and citizenship ceremonies, the issue has been debated by an increasing number of Australian local councils since 2013. Together, these actions have even sparked a heated national debate about whether local governments are overstepping their remit in seeking to govern national values (Bowden and Cunningham, 2017). Notably, the current Prime Minister Scott Morrison and former Prime Minister Malcolm Turnbull have both strongly condemned these so-called "rogue" councils for "playing politics" with the national day; the latter, for instance, accused local governments of "tak[ing] a day that unites Australia and Australians and turn-[ing] it into one that would divide us" (Baker, 2018). The Federal Government even issued an "Australia Day crackdown" in 2017 that revoked citizenship ceremony rights for councils that had rescheduled them, and eventually, in 2019, initiated a new code mandating all councils to hold citizenship ceremonies on January 26 (Karp, 2019). With more local governments nevertheless joining the campaign to change the date each year (Bolger, 2019), Kelly (2018) quite rightly notes that Australia Day only gets "bigger, brighter, more celebratory and stained by the rising tide of culture war hostility." But localized by the actions of these local governments, this is a culture war that now turns increasingly on intensifying community schisms over Australia's national identity and settler colonial history (Davis, 2014).

For comparative purposes, we have identified cases that can be categorized as Responsiveness (Flinders Island), Entrepreneurial Instigation (Yarra), and Hyperactive Responsiveness (Darebin). Two of these – Yarra and Darebin – are located in inner-city Melbourne, within the so-called "latte belt," and were the initial targets of Federal Government crackdown. As progressive counter-culture hubs, they are among the likely suspects of local governments acting on Australia Day; however, as we demonstrate, despite making their respective decisions in quick succession, Sharp's categories help in revealing their differences. As a small rural island community off the northeast coast of Australia's island state Tasmania, our third case of Flinders Island is markedly different yet is the often forgotten pioneer of alternative Australia Day events. In thinking cross-nationally alongside the Columbus Day controversies, it is helpful to categorize these Australian councils' responses through Sharp's typology as this aids in the process of theory building with respect to Australian local government administration of culture war conflicts.

5.1 Australian Local Government Roles in the January 26 Controversy

Before we begin, it is important to underscore some key differences between our two contexts and case studies. Australian local governments are significantly weaker than their American counterparts, as we have already noted. This is something that the Australian Federal Government has capitalized on in responding to local governments that support the Change the Date campaign. The new Australian Citizenship Ceremonies Code (Commonwealth of Australia, 2019) formalizes the financial and administrative penalties nonconforming local governments will bear, and serves as a warning to other councils contemplating challenging the status quo. However, despite their limited powers and the pressure exerted by the Federal Government, selected local governments continue to play similarly responsive roles as their much more powerful American counterparts. Another key difference is that, while a growing number of American states have replaced Columbus Day with Indigenous Peoples' Day, the equivalent action is not applicable in Australia. As a federally mandated public holiday that is equally enforced across Australia's states and territories, local councils are decidedly on their own. In this regard, we can expect that intergovernmental relations will play out fairly differently in the Australian context, with vertical relations to Federal Government simultaneously constraining and politicizing local actions, while horizontal relations are more likely to be influential between sympathetic councils, as well as local government associations and networks. That the reform/nonreformed distinction does not apply to Australian local governments will additionally mean institutional differences, at least in the sense Sharp articulates, will have less explanatory power.

It is also worth elaborating on the Australian cultural context. It is clear that Australia cannot approximate to the immense diversity of the United States; not only is it far smaller (population-wise), but most major cities and towns are geographically situated along or close to the coastline, particularly in the east, with sparser settlement further inland. As might be expected, the overwhelming majority of councils that have taken action on Australia Day are urban councils, located within capital cities or regional centers, although there are some notable exceptions. Similar to the United States, Australian lifestyles, politics, and social values broadly fall within progressive and conservative camps, the fault lines of which are expressed geographically in urban areas (Ting, 2017). Again, while cities in culturally progressive areas have been among the most active on Australia Day, this is not exclusively so.

5.1.1 Flinders Island, Tasmania

Our first case takes us back to late 2013 when Flinders Island Council quietly began a gradual process of cancelling and replacing their traditional Australia Day beach celebrations with a more inclusive event that would bring together local Aboriginal and non-Aboriginal residents to acknowledge the Island's indigenous history (Shine, 2018). A tiny and remote community home to less than 1,000 people, Flinders Island is an unlikely pioneer. Unlike Berkeley, it is not a place of broader cultural influence. Yet a combination of local sentiment, a dark colonial past, and a Council open to reflecting on how its January 26 beach event excluded many of the Island's indigenous residents defined Flinders Island's measured yet resolute response to the Australia Day controversy (Mansell, 2016).

Flinders Island offers a textbook example of Responsiveness in Sharp's formulation. The decision to replace Australia Day celebrations emerged out of a long period of consultation and deliberation. The Council first broached the issue in 2012 in response to the concerns of the local Aboriginal community, initiating a set of workshops – two involving elected members in 2013 – which looked at supporting another event on a day that would be less divisive (Flinders Council, 2013). These consultations resulted in a series of initiatives designed to facilitate a transition away from the January 26 celebration. The first of these was the disbanding of the Australia Day Committee in November 2013, with the Council passing a motion calling on staff to organize and manage an alternative event to be held on the Australia Day weekend (Flinders Council, 2013). Thus, when Flinders Island held its inaugural Furneaux Islands Festival in 2014 – on Saturday January 25 – the scene had already been set for a different approach. The justification for the change was not formulated to "slam something down [anyone's] face," as the current Mayor, Annie Revie, explains (Busbridge and Chou, 2020). Instead, the Council framed the event as one of inclusivity and local pride. Indeed, the former Mayor, Carol Cox, declared in 2014 that 'this Council recognizes the diverse background of Islanders, Aboriginal and European, and has chosen to support a community-initiated event . . . to celebrate being Australian and . . . living in the Furneaux group [of islands], a place of unique beauty and fertile land and sea' (Flinders Council, 2015).

The Council's action flew under the radar until national political and media limelight struck the Australia Day culture war in 2018 (Shine, 2018; Wilkins, 2018). Even so, Flinders Island escaped much of the criticism levelled at other councils – in part because it has not had to deal with the issue of citizenship ceremonies on January 26, given its size (Holmes, 2019). But just as important has been the Council's efforts to depoliticize its decision through a steady, deliberative approach that has involved partnerships with local organizations. This is not to say that it did not receive ire from community members, or that there were not divisions within Council. When the Council first made the decision to replace the traditional beach barbecue, former Deputy Mayor Marc Cobham recalls "there were some fairly ... vehement letters in the local island newspaper" (Shine, 2018). Still, following the success of the 2014 festival, the Council began a partnership with the Flinders Island Aboriginal Association Incorporated (FIAAI) to deliver a more ambitious three-day event to be held in January, celebrating art, food, and indigenous culture. The FIAAI endorsed the event as "a giant step forward to build[ing] positive relationships with Council and the Aboriginal Community" (Flinders Council, 2016b).

In 2016, Flinders Council was presented with a petition with 145 signatories requesting that Council recognize January 26 and hold an appropriate event "to celebrate the occasion of Australia's National Day" (Flinders Council, 2016a). In response, the Council unanimously passed a motion reaffirming that community members were free to celebrate January 26 as they wish and were not precluded from holding their own Australia Day celebrations – but it also committed a minimum of four-years funding to support the Furneaux Islands Festival (Flinders Council, 2016b). Most recently, the Council enshrined its role in delivering the festival in policy, confirming that Council will "manage, coordinate and deliver an annual Furneaux Islands Festival in partnership with the Community" (Flinders Council, 2018).

It is not so much local culture as history that is the defining factor in Flinders Island's decision to replace Australia Day. Certainly, the Island does not fit by any stretch of the imagination the progressive, postindustrial communities that Sharp argues are likely to be most responsive to challenges to the status quo. But, importantly, it has a relatively high Aboriginal population: As Mayor Revie states, "our Indigenous population is 17 per cent [compared to 3 percent nationally] and we don't want to offend that population" (Holmes, 2019). Flinders Island could not have initiated their alternative event without the Aboriginal community who were active in sharing the negative feelings January 26 evoked for them (Mansell, 2016), nor could it have developed a successful festival without the partnership of the FIAAI, which contributes significant financial and staff resources and was instrumental in the push to make the festival a matter of policy (Flinders, 2016b; Holmes, 2019). Furthermore, the Island has a dark and tragic history as a place where, in the 1830s, mainland Aboriginal Tasmanians were exiled by colonial authorities (Shine, 2018). Anti-Aboriginal racism thus has a long heritage among the European community of the Island and has been noted as a persistent social fracture (Mansell, 2016). In this regard, it was community *divisions* and their potential to be inflamed that prompted the Council's responsiveness. It was only through careful, cautious, and prudent deliberation that the Council initiated any change so as not to instigate further or unnecessary tensions within the community.

Sharp's economic explanation further illuminates why, despite the potential for conflict, Flinders Council has been able to create what has ultimately been a point of unification through the Furneaux Islands Festival (Mansell, 2016; Wilkins, 2018). The small population is a consistent point of concern for the Council and the Island's business organizations (Busbridge and Chou, 2020). The Furneaux Islands Festival is a big tourist drawcard, which has the capacity to contribute substantially to the Island's economy. This is a point the Council noted explicitly in its Furneaux Islands Policy, stating that the festival "provides local economic benefit" through its capacity to "stimulate tourism" (Flinders Council, 2018). This finding overlaps with Sharp's; she found that economically declining cities in the United States tend to be particularly wary of status quo challengers when they directly threaten a city's broader economic position or image (Sharp, 2005, p. 126). Where this does not happen or, conversely, where the challenge to the status quo actually contributes to the city's economy, we should expect to see greater support for these causes. This demonstrates that we should not underestimate the significance of economic considerations in community support.

5.1.2 Yarra, Victoria

While Flinders Island has managed to fly under the radar of culture war contestation, our second case represents arguably the most controversial and decisive action on Australia Day taken by a local council to date. Yarra was certainly not the first council to ignite a media storm for its 2017 decision to abandon all events held on January 26, including the citizenship ceremony. The City of Fremantle in Western Australia had received vehement media and political scrutiny when it chose, in 2016, to cancel its annual Australia Day fireworks in favor of an alternative celebration called 'One Day in Fremantle' held close to, but not on, January 26 (Bennett, 2016). But whereas Fremantle was cautioned by the Federal Government against cancelling its Australia Day citizenship ceremony, the City of Yarra took that bold step. Refusing to back down despite strong government pressure, this action remains unprecedented – both in intention and in effect (Wahlquist, 2017).

Yarra's story begins at the end of 2016, following the election of a new Council eager to make its mark among the growing momentum of the Change the Date campaign (Chou and Busbridge, 2019). In February 2017, a councillor motion was carried unanimously to commence discussions with local indigenous residents, representatives, and bodies, namely the Council's Aboriginal Advisory Group (AAG) and the Wurundjeri Tribe Council, on the future of Yarra's Australia Day event and to recommend any changes to be made at the local level (Yarra City Council, 2017a). While the Council was more than eager to move forward as soon as possible, the decision to consult with local indigenous representatives was the result of an intervention by a senior councillor who emphasized the need for Aboriginal perspectives to inform the decision (Yarra City Council, 2017a). The Council-at-large was even more cautious: Council officers took it upon themselves to conduct street surveys with nonindigenous residents as a risk reduction measure, and these were carried out between April and June alongside extensive external consultations with the Aboriginal community (Yarra City Council, 2017b). These consultations revealed that the majority of Aboriginal community members experienced Australia Day as a painful and alienating day, wanted to see the Council support the campaign to Change the Date, and preferred that the Council did not hold any events on January 26 (Yarra City Council, 2017a). Street surveys likewise indicated a strong level of community support for Council recognition of Aboriginal and Torres Strait Islander perspectives on Australia Day (Yarra City Council, 2017a).

The Council unanimously elected to change the way January 26 was commemorated in Yarra in August 2017. The so-called "January 26 Project" entailed a list of recommendations, including that the Council hold a "small-scale, culturally sensitive event . . . on January 26 that acknowledges the loss of culture, language, and identity felt by Aboriginal community"; refer "to January 26 as Australia Day in all communications"; and, most controversially, "cease holding Citizenship Ceremonies on January 26" (Yarra City Council, 2017b, p. 13). Writing in *The Sydney Morning Herald* about Yarra's decision, then Mayor Amanda Stone (2017) noted that Yarra Council "do not believe it is the right day for our national celebration and certainly not the right day to be welcoming our newest citizens to our nation in a citizenship ceremony. This day can only commemorate the British invasion of Aboriginal and Torres Straits Islander lands." Yarra's decision quickly produced a firestorm. The then Prime Minister Malcolm Turnbull labelled the decision "an attack on Australia Day" while state politicians called for the Council to be sacked (Clure, 2017). Within one day, Yarra Council had its rights to officiate citizenship ceremonies stripped (Wahlquist, 2017) – a threat that the Federal Government followed through and that continues to constrain broader local government actions on January 26 (Holmes, 2019).

While the vehement reaction to Yarra's decision surprised almost everyone at the Council (Stone, 2017), what best characterizes this case is not Unintentional

Instigation but Principled Entrepreneurial Instigation. As much as it aligned with Aboriginal and non-Aboriginal community sentiment, and adhered to consultation procedures, the Council's decision to push this contentious issue onto the agenda was not due to a local crisis or petition; rather, the impetus came from councillors themselves. Local subculture is no doubt decisive here. Yarra is an inner-city urban community often considered "hipster central" as well as a stronghold for the progressive Australian Greens party (Economou, 2010; Percy, 2017). Well-known in both the scholarly and popular literature as a hub for countercultural movements and young progressive communities, the suburbs that make up the City of Yarra are widely regarded as "important site[s] of alternative culture, education and creativity" (O'Hanlon and Sharpe, 2009, p. 289). Moreover, Yarra has a strong history as a site of Aboriginal political activism and community organization. Situated on the lands of the Wurundjeri people, the area has historically been an important meeting place for Aboriginal and Torres Strait Islander people and the Council consistently emphasizes its strong commitment to the Aboriginal community (Yarra City Council, 2017b). Through successive Aboriginal Partnership Plans, the Council has recognized the Wurundjeri as the "true sovereigns, caretakers, and custodians of the land" and prides itself as a "local government leader and innovator in promoting Aboriginal history and culture" (Yarra City Council, 2015, pp. 10–11). It is this local subculture that has produced an institutional context where a developed and integrated indigenous representation and recognition exists in the formal structures of the Council.

The intergovernmental context of Yarra's decision is also significant. It is pertinent to reemphasize that Yarra was not entering entirely unchartered territory. Not only did the background of the Council's report on the January 26 Project make mention of Fremantle's decision, it also noted a resolution passed at the National General Assembly of Local Government in 2017 calling on Australian councils to consider efforts they might take in relation to the Australia Day issue (Yarra City Council, 2017b, p. 11). In the absence of state differentiation in celebrating the January 26 public holiday, these horizontal relationships empower action against the status quo and most certainly influenced how Yarra framed its decision. The Victorian *Local Government Act 1989* underscores the "dual function of local government" to be a "service provider and a vehicle of local democratic governance" (Georgio, Davis, and Murphy, 2013, p. 4). According to the Council, the January 26 Project did not just deal with an issue the local community was "looking for leadership on" but was fundamentally about "advocating the interests of the local community to other communities and governments" (Yarra City Council, 2017c). Ever the political entrepreneur, Yarra was fully aware that its decisions would "have a high level of influence on other local governments in Victoria and beyond" (Yarra City Council, 2017c).

5.1.3 Darebin, Victoria

Our last case does not take us very far from Yarra, in either space or time. The City of Darebin not only borders Yarra, but quickly followed its lead on the Australia Day issue. Within the span of a week, and with the political firestorm over Yarra's decision still raging, Darebin Council decided to bring forward a scheduled vote about whether it should cease referring to January 26 as Australia Day and hold an indigenous-themed event in lieu of the annual citizenship ceremony traditionally held on the day (Clure, 2017). Despite a written warning from the Federal Government cautioning the Council against cancelling citizenship ceremonies, Darebin nevertheless voted to support the motion. Few were surprised when the government stripped Darebin of its powers to conduct citizenship ceremonies as it had done in Yarra.

Like Yakima, Darebin's August 2017 decision was swift and made in the interests of "a serious and respectful conversation on when we celebrate Australia Day and the need to change from the hurtful and deeply divisive date of January 26," as Mayor Susan Rennie explains (Rennie, 2019). Yet what produced the greatest consternation in relation to Darebin was its lack of community consultation. While several Darebin councillors, including former Mayor Kim Le Cerf, had voiced support for the Change the Date campaign well before the 2017 motion, the actual decision was not backed by the extensive consultations with indigenous and nonindigenous residents that had defined Yarra's process. Indeed, Darebin Council only consulted with eighty-one residents, or 0.05 percent of the population (Wahlquist, 2017). Shortly after Darebin's decision, it was reported in the media that the Council had only spent two weeks in July 2017 consulting with a very small cross section of local indigenous and nonindigenous residents (Darebin City Council, 2017). Of the limited pool of respondents, 86 percent supported the Council's plan to change the date, 48 percent supported renaming the Australia Day awards the Darebin Community Awards, but only 6 percent were in favor of changing the citizenship ceremony to a different date (Wahlquist, 2017). Additionally, only seven people participated in the indigenous roundtable discussion, which managed to exclude one of the Council's key indigenous elders who went on to publicly air his dissatisfaction with the consultation process (Masanauskas, 2017).

In "short-circuiting normal procedure" (Sharp, 1997), Darebin should therefore be categorized as a case of Hyperactive Responsiveness. Here, subcultural considerations provide a helpful explanation for the Council's hurried decision. Although traditionally less of a countercultural hub than Yarra, Darebin has become increasingly recognized as a "hipster-fied," progressive community that is in the midst of rapid gentrification and a shift to a postindustrial economy (Ting, 2017). At the time of the decision, Mayor Le Cerf defended the Council's decision, saying that Australia Day had been an issue "our community has been aware of for a very long time [with] the Invasion Day rallies [held in nearby central Melbourne] … happening for many years and only growing" (Busbridge and Chou, 2020). Her position was later reinforced by her successor, who responded to the 2019 Federal Government decision to mandate citizenship ceremonies on January 26 by arguing that "Darebin Council's stand on changing the date of Australia Day aligns with the values of our community" (Rennie, 2019).

Intergovernmental factors are also crucial to this case. There are two important issues here. First, Darebin, like Yarra, is located on Wurundjeri land, which meant that the two Councils had been working together with the Wurundjeri Council as traditional custodians. As Mayor Le Cerf explained, this close relationship meant that "when [Yarra] made their decision, we brought ours forward" (Busbridge and Chou, 2020). Second, like Yarra, Darebin is a stronghold of the Australian Greens and, at the time, both City mayors were Greens party members, even appearing together in media interviews (ABC, 2017). Greens supporters are by far the most vocal when it comes to changing Australia Day; a 2018 survey revealed that 54 percent of Greens voters supported changing the date compared to 34 percent of Labor voters, 17 percent of Liberal voters, and 14 percent of One Nation voters (Review Partners, 2018, p. 18). In the wake of the federal decision to strip Yarra and Darebin of their citizenship powers, the area's federal Member of Parliament, Adam Bandt of the Greens, even agreed to personally conduct citizenship ceremonies for the Councils in defiance of the government (ABC, 2017). While the role of party politics in Australian local government remains broadly underexplored (Dewhurst, Grant, and Huuskes, 2018), it is perhaps no surprise that many of the local councils that have decided to change or alter Australia Day events have strong Greens representation.

One final consideration may throw a different light on Sharp's formulation of Hyperactive Responsiveness. Sharp (1996, p. 754) tends to presume that Hyperactive Responsiveness – *too much* responsiveness – means that local governments are playing with fire. As she writes, there are serious risks to community well-being when public officials are "overwhelmed by intense, special interest minorities or themselves committed to moral crusades" (Sharp, 1996, p. 754). Yet, it may also be the case that Hyperactive Responsiveness can be motivated by the opposite intention: to deal with an issue swiftly in order to avoid the potential costs of drawn out conflict. Mayor Le Cerf indicated as much, saying the decision to move the motion forward was

Table 4 Local government action on Australia Day

Case	Action
Flinders Island, Tasmania (2013)	Responsiveness
Yarra, Victoria (2017)	Entrepreneurial Instigation
Darebin, Victoria (2017)	Hyperactive Responsiveness

about seeking "clarity about what our Council might do because it would impact staff and their work given the media attention at the time" (Busbridge and Chou, 2020, p. 19). As for the lack of public consultation, she noted that the Council had been receiving informal feedback from the local indigenous community "for a very long time about Australia Day and what it meant for them" (Busbridge and Chou, 2020, p. 19). Australia Day, she argued, is no different from any other issue where greater weight is placed "on the feedback of the affected community," in this instance, the indigenous community. In this regard, Darebin was perhaps not so much short-circuiting normal procedure as taking a principled stand in support of their indigenous residents. It is relevant to point out that had the Council conducted a full community consultation it would not have altered what happened – the politicization of the Australia Day issue at the federal level at the time would have seen Darebin stripped of its citizenship powers in any case.

5.2 Conclusion

As with the Section 4, Sharp's categories help cut through outward similarities with respect to local council actions (Table 4).

But even more important than the American context, the act of categorizing and explaining Australian local council actions on contentious political issues is one that has the potential to contribute both to scholarly and administrative debates around whether, and in what ways, local governments can engage in overtly political questions about ideology and culture. Currently, research of this nature is lacking in Australia. However, as more local councils around the country wade into these divisive debates and push for change at the local level, a more systematic and comprehensive understanding of what local governments are doing will become essential.

6 Refining Local Governmental Responses to Culture Wars

In this last substantive section, we consider four representative cases that do not fit neatly within existing categories of local government responses before applying Sharp's methodology of conceptual refinement to extend her typology. While we have demonstrated that Sharp's framework of local governmental responses to culture war conflicts can illuminate the many roles local governments play in the Columbus Day and Australia Day controversies – providing a valuable tool of categorization and explanation that can assist scholars and public officials to understand what local governments do – Sharp (1999a; 1999b) herself emphasizes that typologies require updating from time to time in light of new developments. We demonstrate that the ways in which some local governments – Columbus, Ohio; Seattle, Washington; Kingston, Victoria; and Hobart, Tasmania – have dealt with the Columbus Day and Australia Day controversies possess the potential to cast new light on our understandings of responsiveness. As such, we introduce four additional categories of local government responses – Unintentional Responsiveness, Incremental Responsiveness, Nonresponsive Responsiveness, and Local Activism – to identify some of the ways in which culture war conflicts have changed as a result of contemporary social and political developments as well as the shifting dynamics of local government administration and policymaking.

6.1 Columbus, Ohio

It is fitting that a study of Columbus Day should take stock of what its most prominent namesake city has done on the issue. But unlike a Los Angeles, which can be defined by its entrepreneurism, or a Baltimore, which can be characterized by its nonresponsiveness, having debated and then refused to replace Columbus Day with Indigenous Peoples' Day, Columbus made news in 2018 for an altogether different reason. For a city named after Columbus, and which once spent $95 million to celebrate the 500th anniversary of the Italian explorer's voyage to the New World (Flynn, 2018), its October 2018 decision to cancel the holiday on financial grounds is not just ironic. It also requires closer examination.

Columbus's decision to cancel Columbus Day was announced through the Mayor's office via a discreet news release just days before the City was set to mark the holiday in 2018. Noting that City offices would operate as usual, the release declared that "In honor of those who have served in the military, the City of Columbus will be closed on Veteran's Day on Monday, November 12, 2018" (City of Columbus, 2018). A senior spokeswoman for Mayor Andrew Ginther explained the decision: "We chose to close on Veterans Day instead of Columbus Day to honor those who have served our country. In order to be good stewards of taxpayer money, we did not feel it was prudent to add an additional paid holiday" (Flynn, 2018). The decision had less to do with the politics surrounding Columbus Day than the fact that Columbus is home to many veterans. "We have a number of veterans who work for the city, and there are so many here in Columbus. We thought it was important to honor them with that day off," explained the Mayor's spokeswoman (Perez, 2018). Moreover, when asked whether the City had made the change through a process of open public debate, she added that the decision had been "agreed upon by all of the unions that represent city workers during regular contract negotiations over the last year" (Chappell, 2018). Despite this, organizers of the annual Columbus Italian Festival said the City did not include them in any consultation or give them advanced notice of the decision (Carr Smyth, 2018).

On the basis of these facts, Columbus's decision to abandon Columbus Day is distinctive in two key respects. First, the City's decision was not officially influenced by the growing movement to replace Columbus Day with Indigenous Peoples' Day. With no explicit mention of Indigenous Peoples' Day in the Mayor's news release, the City instead made the "savvy move," in the words of one commentator, "to tie the switch to a politically safe demographic: veterans" (Carr Smyth, 2018). What motivated their decision was not the rejection of Columbus Day to embrace Indigenous Peoples' Day. Rather, the decision simply redirected the City's budget to another cause – veterans – which had long been celebrated in Columbus. In fact, Columbus is home to one of "the nation's biggest [Veterans Day] parades," according to the Department of Defense (City of Columbus, 2013). However, in so doing, the City became embroiled in a conflict it had no intention of igniting.

Second, the City's decision to replace Columbus Day with Veterans Day was driven by financial rather than cultural considerations. In justifying the decision, the Mayor's spokeswoman said that the City did not have the budget to give its 8,500 employees two holidays, and this was why they chose Veterans Day given Columbus's large veteran population (Carr Smyth, 2018). But again, by siding with the City's veteran population to recognize Veterans Day, Columbus found itself at the center of the growing controversy surrounding the cultural meaning of the Columbus Day holiday.

6.2 Kingston, Victoria

Though located in faraway Australia, across Melbourne's southeast suburbs, our next case – Kingston, Victoria – was likewise motivated by budgetary concerns when it decided to cancel one of its customary January 26 events, the Globe to Globe World Music Festival, in 2018. Like Columbus, Kingston's decision to discontinue the January 26 festival was attributed, along with several other festivals scheduled during the year, to rising recycling costs

(Kingston City Council, 2018). But the motion in which these changes were proposed, and carried, also moved that the "format and focus" of the Australia Day Breakfast – Kingston's other January 26 event – should "have a greater emphasis on the Citizenship ceremony while retaining the Citizen and Community Group of the Year Awards as the key awards to be presented at the event to be held on Australia Day at the Kingston City Hall" (Kingston City Council, 2018).

Outwardly, important overlaps exist between the decisions of Columbus and Kingston. Both cities decided, for financial reasons, to de-emphasize a holiday in order to recognize another cause or issue. But one significant difference separates these two cities' actions. In Kingston's case, while cost cutting was the official rationale for abandoning the January 26 festival, the decision represented a first step for a minority of councillors to move the City away from holding any form of celebration on Australia Day. Councillor Steve Staikos, a long-serving representative of the City, explained his own motivations this way:

> I had been thinking for a long time about how to move the Globe to Globe Festival away from Australia Day. I think it is a festival that needs to stand on its own and it needs to celebrate diversity . . . .But then one of our councilors on the conservative side basically said he wanted to cancel a bunch of festivals to save money because of recycling costs. So, the other councilors said, "okay, we'll agree to that at this point in time." But I've got a little plan to bring back the festival next year when the crunch isn't as bad and to have it on a different weekend. Ultimately, I would like to see our Australia Day event shrink down to basically a citizenship ceremony. (Busbridge and Chou, 2020, p. 24)

Kingston's decision thus represents something quite different to Columbus – and to other Australian local councils for that matter. Rather than a direct response to the Australia Day controversy, it represented an indirect and largely discreet one that was undetected by culture warriors. For Councillor Staikos, budgetary considerations presented an ideal first step in an incremental process. As he explains:

> We are a middle-suburban Council with very middle-class suburbs and very moderate political views. So, we haven't really been on the cutting-edge or at the forefront of social change because, by and large, the City of Kingston has been dominated by conservatives. That's why any change will always be slow and soft. We'll change things our way. We don't want to do it by storming the Bastille . . . I'm trying to shift Council slowly so that it doesn't create a knee-jerk reaction in the community. (Busbridge and Chou, 2020, p. 24)

Unlike many other councils in Australia, Kingston has not hit the headlines. But that does not mean it has been inactive. To the contrary, the Council's actions have been framed by the recognition that, in certain contexts, controversial and divisive issues are best addressed slowly, discreetly, and through a process of policy evolution rather than revolution.

6.3 Hobart, Tasmania

Hobart, Tasmania's capital, may be located in the same state as Flinders Island, but the two councils' respective Australia Day decisions could not be more different. Put simply, Hobart City Council's October 2017 decision to retain the City's January 26 Australia Day events *and* formally join the campaign to Change the Date can only be described as contradictory (Browning, 2017). Through a four-point motion, passed by a 7–2 vote, the Council committed itself to the "non-politicisation" of January 26 events while moving to "officially support a change of date for Australia Day" (Hobart City Council, 2017a). This entailed "supporting and becoming part of the national #changethedate campaign" as well as "joining with other Australian councils that support a change of date from 26 January, to lobby the Australian government" (Hobart City Council, 2017a). Locally, it also moved to back any Council members who wished to participate in the Invasion Day protest led by the Tasmanian Aboriginal Community and compelled the Council to support Invasion Day events and rallies.

The Council's decision was quickly labeled by one City aldermen as having a "bob each way" (Thomas-Wilson, 2017). As a response to the Australia Day controversy, Hobart's decision thus represented an instance of a Council wanting to have their cake and eat it too. But, though contradictory, a closer look at the Council's decision makes clear that Hobart was trying to balance two opposing objectives. On the one hand, the Council was officially committed to the "non-politicisation and continuation of all citizenship ceremonies" on January 26 because it did not want the Federal Government to strip it of its right to confer citizenship ceremonies (Browning, 2017). As Alderman Bill Harvey explained, "we wouldn't like to see the citizenship ceremonies, which we all believe are really important, taken away from us like it has occurred in a couple of other mainland councils" (Browning, 2017). On the other hand, this did not mean that the Council did not want to take leadership on the Australia Day issue. As was noted in the Council Report on the matter, there was notable public feedback supporting the "Council's move in taking a leadership role in this debate" (Hobart City Council, 2017b). On the whole, Council was broadly supportive of the movement to change the date (Thomas-Wilson, 2017). Indeed, it was Hobart City Council that rallied other local governments around the country to lobby the Federal Government about changing Australia Day at the 2017 National General Assembly of Local Government, a motion that passed by 64–62 votes (Whitson, 2017).

It was the balancing of these two different priorities, according to Helen Burnet, the alderman who submitted the motion to reconsider the City's January 26 events, that led the Council to adopt the contradictory decision that it did. As she put it:

> The rule is that if a local council wants to have a citizenship ceremony, it's done on the terms of the federal government and the federal government was not interested in changing Australia Day from January 26. Our Council was very committed to recognizing the citizenship ceremony and therefore didn't want to lose that right ... [B]ut it didn't mean that we didn't also want to recognize and try and work towards another day for Australia Day. That desire was still really important for us. (Busbridge and Chou, 2020, pp. 24–25)

In doing this, Hobart broadly refused to make policy that would shift the status quo – locally, at least. Instead, it set its sights far wider, targeting the national status quo by supporting the Change the Date movement.

6.4 Seattle, Washington

Our final case takes us back to the United States – to Seattle, the first city in Washington state to replace Columbus Day with Indigenous Peoples' Day. Seattle's case is straightforward in many respects. In response to local activism, the City Council unanimously voted in 2014 to support "an opportunity to celebrate the thriving cultures and values of the Indigenous Peoples of our region" (Goodman, 2014; Seattle City Council, 2014). Although sections of Seattle's Italian-American community felt "deeply offended," the Council thought it necessary to turn away from a figure who had "played such a pivotal role in the worst genocide humankind has ever known" (Beekman, 2014).

However, a closer look at Seattle highlights a fair bit more than a simple case of governmental responsiveness. While socialist council member Kshama Sawant, as one of the resolution's sponsors, quickly become the public face of Seattle's push to replace Columbus Day, working behind the scenes was a prominent local activist, Matt Remle, who had in fact drafted the resolution passed by the Council. A Seattle resident of Lakota heritage and Native American liaison at Marysville-Pilchuck High School, Remle had been actively trying to rename Columbus Day since the late 1990s, when he began working with the Duwamish Tribe to stop the Council bringing in replicas of Columbus's ships (KEXP, 2018). Then, in 2011, he had his lightbulb moment. As he explains:

The origins for both the Seattle city council and Seattle school board resolutions date back to 2011, when I was attending an Abolish Columbus Day rally in downtown Seattle. As I was listening to the beautiful songs of a local canoe family, I started thinking about South Dakota and their successful effort to change Columbus Day to Native American Day. That night I decided to contact members of the Seattle city council as well as my local State Legislatures to see if they might be willing to do something similar on either the City or State level. (Remle, 2014)

Remle quickly became an unofficial go-between on the issue for local Native communities, activist organizations, and local government. His strategy was to target the "local, city, state and tribal levels," ensuring that Tribal Government, City Council, and the School Board were all committed to the cause (Remle, 2018). Understanding that these various domains were connected, and that change had to occur in all domains for change to occur at all, he kept pressure on the City's School Board to "follow through on their commitment" and further ensure City Council made good on efforts to "bring in that tribal voice to the city" to further the relationships between the two communities (Nagle, 2014).

Remle found a close ally in Sawant who could take the fight to the City Council. In a public statement he issued supporting Sawant's 2019 reelection, Remle (2019) recalled that:

When we reached out to Kshama with the Indigenous Peoples Day resolution, we actually had been trying for years in this city, multiple years, in liberal Seattle, to get a resolution to replace Columbus Day with Indigenous Peoples Day, and we were met with silence, literally silence. Until she was elected, and I want to say you responded back within a couple of hours, and said "that's what we got elected for, to support communities, to support oppressed communities, and we will absolutely take on this issue."

Since then, Sawant has partnered with Remle and Mazaska Talks, an umbrella organization fighting for indigenous rights that Remle founded, to push several more contentious issues through the Council: the most controversial being Seattle's decision to divest $3 billion from Wells Fargo bank because of its support for the Dakota Access Pipeline. Just as he did for the Indigenous Peoples' Day cause, Remle drafted the resolution that Sawant moved through Council (Tobias, 2017). Together, Remle and Sawant – who remain very different individuals, working for very different institutions – represent a growing movement of local leaders who increasingly understand that multi-sectoral networks and platforms linking local government with civic and private sector partners are the new normal for those seeking to solve entrenched problems and effect lasting change.

6.5 Conceptual Refinement

These four cases represent a cross section of a diverse set of local government responses to the Columbus Day and Australia Day culture wars that Sharp's existing categories cannot fully explain. Yet, we contend that there is enough in each that is representative of entirely new categories of local government roles in cultural controversies and new grounds for theorizing why local governments govern culture war conflicts in the ways they do.

6.5.1 Unintentional Responsiveness

Columbus's discreet decision to replace Columbus Day with Veterans Day illustrates that governmental decisions can sometimes produce unintended outcomes or be construed in an unintended manner. Despite not intending to wade into the Columbus Day battle, Columbus's actions – influenced by budgetary concerns and a desire to acknowledge the City's veteran population – nevertheless saw it swept up in the culture war controversy over the contentious October holiday. While somewhat inevitable given that it occurred at the height of cities making that precise move on political grounds, it points to something critical: The timing of decisions is often enough to implicate local governments in unwanted causes. Had Columbus made its decision a decade earlier, before the movement to replace Columbus Day took off, it may have averted the community backlash and media coverage it received.

Of course, it is possible to construe Columbus's response simply as an instance of a policy paradox that captures how policy solutions can sometimes seem to be embedded in the very problem they are seeking to resolve, because politics cannot be divorced from policymaking (Stone, 2012). Yet we contend that the Columbus case demonstrates that a new category – Unintentional Responsiveness – is required to explain what transpired. This is because in responding to the City's veteran population and acknowledging them with their own holiday, Columbus also unintentionally responded to the movement to abandon Columbus Day. While this new category shares key similarities with Unintentional Instigation in the sense that the local government will have no intention of triggering or exacerbating a culture war conflict through their action, it is ultimately not characterized by evasive or repressive measures, or even measures broadly responsive to challenges to the status quo. To the contrary, the defining trait of Unintentional Responsiveness is the interlinking of issues and causes so that by responding to a particular issue, one inadvertently becomes implicated in another cause.

In this way, what we define here as Unintentional Responsiveness is different to how the concept is conventionally construed in the literature. Typically, "unintentional" or "accidental" responsiveness encompasses situations where a representative or government body delivers high-quality representation despite either having no intention of doing so or, alternatively, having a "distaste for representing the will of the people" (Markowski, 2011, p. 2304). Unlike such definitions, where there is no intention to be responsive at all, our definition encompasses two instances of responsiveness: the intended response (concerning a nonculture war issue) and the unintended response (concerning a culture war issue).

Although this category of response might be attributed to poor or imprudent policymaking on the part of local government, it may also be an indirect consequence of what policy scholars such as Baumgartner and Jones (1993) call a "punctuated equilibrium" where policy stasis is disrupted by new ideas, alternative approaches, or, in our case, emerging culture war contentions (Thomson, 2010). During these periods when the status quo gives way to rapid policy change, particular policy solutions to entrenched problems can quickly catch fire as a result of shifting governmental will, media attention, and public opinion. When this occurs, actions and policies that once slipped under the radar, were deemed unrealistic, or touched upon ostensibly separate concerns can sometimes be swept up by the mass political momentum and absorbed into the ensuing heated ideological debates and proposed policy shifts. This may be one way to understand the conditions that transform Responsiveness into Unintentional Responsiveness.

To return to the Columbus example: Without the broader local culture war over Columbus Day, Columbus's decision would very likely have been construed in quite a different manner, that is, as a budgetary decision to celebrate one holiday over another. But that it was reached at the height of debates over the contentious October holiday – when stability had been punctuated by the flood of cities replacing Columbus Day with Indigenous Peoples' Day – meant that its decision was seen as part of the spectrum of policy solutions that local governments were offering in response to the cultural legacy embodied by the Italian explorer. As politics becomes more mediatized in the age of populism, instances of Unintentional Instigation might become increasingly common.

6.5.2 Incremental Responsiveness

Our second proposed category – Incremental Responsiveness – speaks to the movement at Kingston to slowly change Australia Day through a process of evolution rather than revolution. Sitting at the other end of the policymaking spectrum from policies made during punctuated equilibria, we argue that local government responsiveness to contentious issues is, more often than not, constrained by "bureaucratic rules, norms, structures, or cultures" (Bryer, 2007, p. 485). Indeed, even where the political will to act exists, councillors often still find themselves constrained by local governmental norms and the cultural views of those they represent. Risk averse administrators may thus prefer a different path to policy entrepreneurs. Instead of openly pushing for rapid wholesale policy change, they may instead opt for small, incremental policy shifts over a long period of time. Lindblom (1959, p. 86) aptly described the process as follows: "A wise policy-maker consequently expects that his policies will achieve only part of what he hopes and at the same time will produce unanticipated consequences he would have preferred to avoid. If he proceeds through a *succession* of incremental changes, he avoids serious lasting mistakes in several ways."

In their analysis of Lindblom's conceptualization of incrementalism, Mintrom and Norman (2009, p. 655) appear to touch upon the very sentiment Councillor Staikos expressed: "Patient actors who hold a clear vision of the end they are seeking can still move policy in directions they desire. The key is to see how a series of small changes could, over time, produce similar results as more dramatic, immediate change." This is a path that can minimize the possibility of conflict expansion which, according to Schattschneider (1960), can come when overt political activism engenders even greater conflict or debate and thus further exacerbates tensions. Given this, less publicized and seemingly more piecemeal actions can often be more effective in advancing contentious political causes (Haider-Markel and Meier, 1996).

Unlike the categories of Responsiveness, Hyperactive Responsiveness, and Symbolic Responsiveness, Incremental Responsiveness sees local governments or councillors play the long game in addressing contentious, culture war type issues. In recognition of the fact that the vast majority of local governments – particularly in Australia – still see their mandates as limited, we argue that it is necessary to establish a category that acknowledges the gradual and often indirect ways that local councils can respond to culturally divisive issues. While there may be no spectacle or immediate evidence of change, Incremental Responsiveness encapsulates the everyday, mundane politics that is more prevalent in local government. In many communities where residents are more politically conservative or centrist, there may be little appetite for local government to spend time advocating for ideological and cultural change. Under these conditions, governments or councillors can nevertheless respond positively to status quo challengers, albeit in an incremental fashion.

6.5.3 Nonresponsive Responsiveness

The third category we propose – Nonresponsive Responsiveness – speaks to Hobart's seemingly contradictory decision to retain its Australia Day celebrations while backing the Change the Date campaign and supporting council members wishing to participate in the Invasion Day protest. By doing this, Hobart effectively adopted both a Nonresponsive and Responsive stance on the Australia Day issue.

However, what appears at first glance to be contradictory, if not confused, policymaking may be construed another way in the context of culture wars. After all, culture wars are defined by a polarized culture where political common ground seems a remote possibility. "A society experiencing a culture war," writes Thomson (2010, p. 12) "would lack common standards and assumptions, and as a result, the ability to make public policy decisions would be severely compromised." Under these circumstances, public policies can either explicitly pander only to orthodox or progressive views, and in so doing alienate and anger the other side, or it can seek compromise, however uncomfortable, temporary, and imperfect it is. The former approach might particularly appeal to culture war warriors or those, as George (2009, p. 7) contends, who "are engaged in protracted competition for cultural hegemony – for the hearts and minds of the great majority of people and for the levers of power by which the dominant culture might operationalise its images of the 'good' life." For such political actors, engaging in "wedge politics" and dividing the population is the modus vivendi (McKnight, 2005, p. 140). However, if the desire is to resolve culture war conflicts, then the latter approach may be preferred. Here, the first step may simply be to ease tensions, where possible. Given that culture wars typically denote deep struggles over first principles, it is unlikely that one policy can adequately appease or satisfy all parties. Instead, in recognition of the fact that policymaking on contested issues about ideology and culture often boils down to balancing competing political claims, which are difficult if impossible to reconcile, sometimes all that local governments can do is to proceed in a seemingly contradictory fashion that allows them to, as it were, have a foot in each camp.

Technically, Nonresponsive Responsiveness is a subcategory of negotiated responsiveness whereby administrators and policymakers "seek balance between multiple, potentially competing demands" as a mechanism of conflict resolution (Bryer, 2007, p. 488). Part of this balancing act requires officials to accommodate both the interests and actions of the various competing parties. Although local governments have always had to respond to diverse groups (Buchanan and Tullock, 1965), these demands can be especially pronounced in respect of culture war issues. This may account for why Hobart responded both to those who support Australia Day and wanted it recognized through the City's citizenship ceremony and celebrations as well as those who support the Change the Date campaign and felt it important to demonstrate as part of the

Invasion Day protest. It may also be why it ultimately refused to shift the status quo locally while setting its sights on national change.

6.5.4 Local Activism

The Seattle case leads us to our final proposed category: Local Activism. Why Seattle interests us is that it is representative of a new localism wherein "multisectoral networks ... work together to solve problems" that require fluid collaboration between a range of "civic and private sector partners" (Katz and Nowak, 2017, p. 10). Just like their state and federal counterparts, local governments are embedded in, and influenced by, extensive networks of public, private, and nonprofit sectors and organizations. The movement to replace Columbus Day with Indigenous Peoples' Day has come to epitomize the extent to which local activists and local government now depend upon, cooperate with, and pressure each other in order to effect lasting cultural change both within and beyond city hall. We make this claim despite Seattle being a mayor-council system, which tends to be "less responsive to minority concerns and ... to engage in less symbolic policy making" (Taylor, Haider-Markel, and Lewis, 2018a; see also, Taylor et al. 2014; Taylor, Haider-Markel, and Lewis, 2018b). This is because the type of Local Activism we advance here is less akin to more conventional forms of activism than to a type of networked governance that seeks to implement practices of collective cogoverning – between elected local officials, community businesses, civic organizations, academic leaders, and local residents – to solve community challenges. Such activist networks draw in and work with both governmental and nongovernmental actors who are eager to advance particular political causes.

Specifically, when it comes to Local Activism, there are both old and new developments that are worth highlighting. First, what we label here as Local Activism is closely linked to the concept of advocacy coalitions. According to Sabatier (1988, p. 131), policy change will increasingly not come from "any specific governmental institution" but from a "policy subsystem, i.e. those actors from a variety of public and private organizations who are actively concerned with a policy problem or issue." Moreover, instead of the "traditional triangles" of administrative agencies, legislative committees, and interest groups at a single level of government, contemporary policy subsystems "include actors at various levels of government active in policy formulation and implementation, as well as journalists, researchers, and policy analysts who play important roles in the generation, dissemination, and evaluation of policy ideas" (Sabatier, 1988, p. 131). In any such subsystem, advocacy coalitions comprised of individuals from various public, private, and nonprofit organizations will form; these can help drive initiatives forward in numerous forums. For Stoker (2011), many local governments long ago adopted such a networked approach to public administration. In an increasingly complex and interconnected world, local governments appreciate that the "task of community governance demands a diverse set of relationships with 'higher' tier government, local organizations and stakeholders and citizens" (Stoker, 2011, p. 17). These relationships can form in any city regardless of the institutional setting.

At the same time, the Local Activism we highlight also encompasses some new political developments. One of the more interesting developments in federal political systems is the "drifting downward [of power] from the nation-state to cities and metropolitan communities" and "horizontally from government to networks of public, private, and civic actors" (Katz and Nowak, 2017, p. 1). According to Katz and Nowak (2017, p. 10), this so-called new localism is distinctive insofar as it is not restricted solely to the work of local government but encompasses "multisectoral networks that work together to solve problems." Particularly at a time when national political leaders and parties have proven themselves incapable of addressing today's key political, economic, social, and environmental challenges, more and more actors at the bottom of the federal hierarchy have risen to engage in ideological battles, using a variety of tools – both through and around government – in order to redress pressing problems in their own communities. New localism is not without its critics (Grant and Drew, 2017). Even so, it underscores the reality in which many contemporary local governments, activists, and organizations find themselves.

These dynamics are not adequately recognized by Sharp's framework, which tends to see local governments as largely independent governmental entities separated from the local activists, or status quo challengers, who push culture war controversies onto the local government agenda from time to time. Yet our study demonstrates that this view of local government needs to be revised. Accordingly, we argue that a category of local governmental response is necessary to capture this new localism whereby local government and councillors see themselves as empowered to tackle big issues, both through formal and informal governmental and nongovernmental networks. While this category of Local Activism will necessarily involve political entrepreneurship, it differs from Sharp's category of Entrepreneurial Instigation in two important respects. First, while Entrepreneurial Instigation mostly entails local governmental responses that support status quo culture war challengers on principled grounds, Local Activism can involve a range of responses to culture war conflicts, from Evasion and Responsiveness to Instigation. Second, and most importantly,

Table 5 Local government action on Columbus Day and
Australia Day

Case	Action
Columbus, Ohio (2018)	Unintentional Responsiveness
Kingston, Victoria (2018)	Incremental Responsiveness
Hobart, Tasmania (2017)	Nonresponsive Responsiveness
Seattle, Washington (2014)	Local Activism

while Entrepreneurial Instigation is primarily limited to local government
action, Local Activism sees local government and councillors work with and
outside government, too.

6.6 Conclusion

The four new categories of local government responses highlighted by the four
cases discussed in this section (Table 5) have resonance with existing ideas in
the public policy and public administration literatures, which means they are not
exclusively applicable to culture wars. Bringing these to bear on culture war
clashes is a pertinent reminder that divisive issues are part of the everyday
business of local governance and subjects of policy and administrative concern.

Doing so also affords us a helpful means to further arbitrate the different roles
local governments can, and do, play in contentious ideological and moral
debates. In summary, the defining traits of each of these new categories are as
follows:

(a) Unintentional Responsiveness – a response to a non-culture war issue that
is subsequently framed in terms of culture war;
(b) Incremental Responsiveness – a series of small, unremarkable decisions
that are intended to facilitate, over time, dramatic shifts to the status quo;
(c) Nonresponsive Responsiveness – local status quo unchanged but other
steps are taken in favor of status quo challengers;
(d) Local Activism – local government responses to culture war issues embedded in, and shaped by, multisectoral networks of other governments, civil
society, private, and nonprofit institutions and actors.

7 Conclusion

Integrating these four new categories into Sharp's typology does not just enlarge
our understanding of the variety of roles local governments can play in moral
and cultural controversies. It also paints a slightly different picture of the social,

Table 6 Updated typology of local government roles in culture war conflicts

Response	Not supportive of status quo challengers	Ambiguous responsiveness to status quo challengers	Supportive of status quo challengers
First-order	Evasion	**Incremental Responsiveness**	Responsiveness
	Agenda Denial	**Nonresponsive Responsiveness**	Hyperactive Responsiveness
	Repression		Symbolic Responsiveness
	Nonresponsiveness		Entrepreneurial Instigation
	Local Activism		**Local Activism**
Second-order	Unintentional Instigation	**Unintentional Responsiveness**	Unintentional Instigation

cultural, and political circumstances they must navigate when they take action on such issues, bringing into clearer view the particularities of contemporary culture war conflicts and the unique challenges they pose for local governance, policymaking, and administration. We thus conclude this Element with three key reflections on our extension of Sharp's original typology of local governmental responses (Table 6). Updating her categories illuminates some of the implicit assumptions undergirding her conceptions of local government and culture wars. This is not just exceptionally useful in advancing the paradigm more generally but also for honing in on what precisely has changed as a result of contemporary populist politics and shifts toward decentralization.

First, unlike Sharp's typology where local governments are either supportive or unsupportive of culture war challengers to the status quo, our updated version introduces *ambiguity* as an additional point of distinction in local governmental responses. The two new categories of Incremental Responsiveness and Nonresponsive Responsiveness encompass cases where local governments are neither fully supportive nor fully unsupportive of status quo challengers, either seeking slow change that happens behind the scenes or adopting seemingly contradictory policy agendas. These should not be considered anomalous categories, but instead par for the course in culture wars, where heavy politicization can constrain the capacity or willingness of local governments to settle on one side of the fence or the other. Cases of ambiguous responsiveness will be more likely in particularly explosive culture war issues, where local government powers are limited, or in communities that are more conservative and resistant to change. In these contexts, the legal, financial, political, and symbolic costs associated with culture wars may simply be too great for local governments to bear, making ambiguous, seemingly contradictory, or behind the scenes action more likely. Recognizing that responses to cultural, moral, and ideological controversies are not always clear-cut allows a greater appreciation of the contingencies of culture war struggles and highlights some of the less inflammatory options available to local governments that may be dealing with considerable politicization.

Second, our incorporation of Unintentional Responsiveness as a - possible second-order response highlights the *politicized* character of culture war disputes in a way that is not always evident in Sharp's original formulation. Second-order responses emerge through the "interactive effects" of government decisions and other parties involved in a particular controversial issue; for Sharp, instigation is the primary unintended outcome of local government action. Introducing responsiveness as an additional unintended, albeit ambiguous, outcome acknowledges how a response to a nonculture war issue can become enfolded within a culture war one, implicating a local government in a controversy in which it had not intended to play a role. (While we do not explore it in this Element, we may surmise that the reverse may be true: that a government may be unintentionally *nonresponsive* to a culture war issue due to previous policy or administrative decisions.) "Culture wars," it must be recalled, is not so much a descriptive category as a polemical one: Led by national elites and propagated by the media, culture war controversies can envelop a variety of actors and issues within the logic of polarization. As more local governments stake a claim on national ideological debates, we might expect this type of unintentional responsiveness to become more common as their actions are subject to greater political and media scrutiny.

Lastly, the addition of the Local Activism category to supportive and unsupportive local governmental responses builds a more robust typology that acknowledges that activism does not necessarily correlate with responsiveness. More importantly, however, it designates local government as part of *multisectoral networks* linking a variety of governmental and nongovernmental actors, partners, and institutions. In this regard, Local Activism is less a straightforwardly descriptive category that explains what local governments do in relation to culture war issues and more an evocative one that points toward: (a) who they do it with and (b) the types of perceptions of local government that undergird such actions. This is a significant shift that goes beyond Sharp's implicit presentation of local governments as effectively independent entities. For Sharp, local governments tend to play more reactive roles in culture wars, becoming implicated when clashes emerge in their jurisdictions or, alternatively, when their decisions on resourcing and administration ignite local divisions. The Local Activism category challenges these assumptions, highlighting an as of yet understudied change in how many local governments and public administrators view their roles in controversies concerning culture, values, and identity. In advancing our understanding of how local governments govern culture wars today, this Element represents a step toward appreciating this important shift. While these insights form part of a broader ongoing research agenda, we hope our study makes a distinct contribution to the literature and provides a practical guide for local government officials now grappling with contentious political conflicts in their own communities.

Bibliography

ABC (2017, August 22) Darebin Council Stripped of Citizenship Ceremony After Controversial Vote. *ABC News.* www.abc.net.au/news/2017-08-22/dar ebin-council-stripped-of-power-to-hold-citizenship-ceremony/8830126.

Altmann, E., Coates, L., and Woods, M. (2018, May 24). Councils' Help with Affordable Housing Shows How Local Government Can Make a Difference. *The Conversation.* https://theconversation.com/councils-help-with-affordable-housing-shows-how-local-government-can-make-a-difference-94739.

American Indian Movement (1994, October 8). An Open Letter from the American Indian Movement of Colorado and Our Allies. *Rocky Mountain News.*

Antonisch, M. (2018). Living in Diversity: Going Beyond the Local/National Divide. *Political Geography,* 63, 1–9.

Appelbaum, Y. (2012, October 8). How Columbus Day Fell Victim to Its Own Success. *The Atlantic.* www.theatlantic.com/national/archive/2012/10/how-columbus-day-fell-victim-to-its-own-success/261922/.

Arnold, M. (1992, October 11). In Bay Area, Columbus Day Runs Aground. *Los Angeles Times.* www.latimes.com/archives/la-xpm-1992–10-11-mn -456-story.html.

Aulich, C. and Pietsch, R. (2002). Left on the Shelf: Local Government and the Australia Constitution. *Australia Journal of Public Administration,* 61(4), 14–23.

Bain, J. G. (2010) Culture Wars. In M. Ryan (ed.), *The Encyclopedia of Literary and Cultural Theory Volume III: Cultural Theory, A-Z.* John Wiley and Sons. http://doi.org/10.1002/9781444337839.

Bain, K. (2016, October 4). Yakima Drops Columbus Day for Indigenous Peoples' Day. *Yakima Herald.* www.yakimaherald.com/news/local/yakima-drops-columbus-day-for-indigenous-people-s-day/article_6b7d6db8-8a8d-11e6-ac5b-8b838ff5af4a.html.

Baker, N. (2018, January 15). "Debate History, Don't Deny It": Turnbull Disappointed by Calls to Change Australia Day. *SBS News.* www.sbs.com .au/news/debate-history-don-t-deny-it-turnbull-disappointed-by-calls-to-change-australia-day.

Barron, D. J. (2003). Reclaiming Home Rule. *Harvard Law Review,* 116(8), 2255–2386.

Baumgartner, F. R. and Jones. B. D. (1993). *Agendas and Instability in American Politics.* Chicago, IL: University of Chicago Press.

Beekman, D. (2014, October 6). Native Americans Cheer City's New Indigenous Peoples' Day. *Seattle Times.* www.seattletimes.com/seattle-news /native-americans-cheer-cityrsquos-new-indigenous-peoplesrsquo-day/.

Bell, P. (2006). How Local Government Can Save Australia's Federal System. In A. J. Brown and J. A. Bellamy (eds.), *Federalism and Regionalism in Australia: New Approaches, New Institutions?* (171–184). Canberra: Australian National University E-Press.

Bennett, C. (2016, November 28). WA Premier Colin Bennett calls Fremantle "Disloyal" for Axing Australia Day Celebrations. *ABC News.* www.abc.net.au/news/2016-11-27/colin-barnett-on-row-over-fremantle-delaying-australia-day/8061644.

Berkeley Indigenous Peoples Day Pow Wow. (n. d.). *The History of Indigenous Peoples Day.* www.ipdpowwow.org/IPD%20History.html.

Berman, D. R. (2003). *Local Government and the States: Autonomy, Politics, and Policy.* Armonk, NY: M. E. Sharpe.

Board, E. (2017, October 17). Reflections on the Columbus Day Culture Wars. *Los Angeles Daily News.* www.dailynews.com/2017/10/17/reflections-on-the-columbus-day-culture-wars/.

Bolger, R. (2019, 14 November). Sydney's Inner West Council Scraps Australia Day Celebrations to Recognise Indigenous Australians. *SBS News.* www.sbs.com.au/news/sydney-s-inner-west-council-scraps-australia-day-celebrations-to-recognise-indigenous-australians.

Borer, M. (2006). The Location of Culture: The Urban Culturalist Approach. *City & Community,* 5(2), 173–197.

Bowden, E. and Cunningham, M. (2017, September 19). Yes, Councils Can Snub Australia Day, Ban Fizzy Drinks and Plastic Bags. *The Age.* www.theage.com.au/national/victoria/yes-councils-can-snub-australia-day-ban-fizzy-drinks-and-plastic-bags-20170919-gyk59p.html.

Brookes, S. (2018) What Do We Mean When We Talk about Populism? Local Politics, Global Movements and "The People" in Political Coverage of the 2016 Australian Federal and United States Federal Elections. *Media, Culture & Society,* 40(8), 1252–1269.

Brooks, D. (2018, July 30). The Third-Party Option. *New York Times.* www.nytimes.com/2018/07/30/opinion/third-party-2020-election-localism.html.

Brown, A. J. (2006). Federalism, Regionalism and the Reshaping of Australian Governance. In A. J. Brown and J. A. Bellamy (eds.), *Federalism and Regionalism in Australia: New Approaches, New Institutions?* (11–32). Canberra: Australian National University E-Press.

Brown, A. J. (2008). In Pursuit of the Genuine Partnership: Local Government and Federal Constitutional Reform in Australia. *UNSW Law Journal,* 31(2), 435–466.

Brown, M., Knopp, L., and Morrill, R. (2005). The Culture Wars and Urban Electoral Politics: Sexuality, Race, and Class in Tacoma, Washington. *Political Geography*, 24(4), 267–291.

Browning, S. (2017, October 24). Hobart City Council Gets behind Campaign for Date Change. *ABC*. www.abc.net.au/news/2017-10-24/hobart-city-council-back-australia-day-date-change/9078100.

Bryer, T. A. (2007). Towards a Relevant Agenda for Responsive Public Administration. *Journal of Public Administration Research*, 17(3), 479–500.

Buchanan, J. M. and Tullock, G. (1965). *The Calculus of Consent: Logical Foundations of Constitutional Democracy*. Ann Arbor, MI: University of Michigan Press.

Busbridge, R. and Chou, M. (2020). Culture Wars and City Politics, Revisited: Local Councils and the Australia Day Controversy. *Urban Affairs Review*. https://doi.org/10.1177/1078087420945034.

Buscaino, J., Cedillo, G., Ryu, D., and Englander, M. (2017, June 14). Letter to the Rules, Elections, Intergovernmental Relations & Neighborhoods Committee. *Los Angeles City Council*. https://cityclerk.lacity.org/lacityclerk connect/index.cfm?fa=ccfi.viewrecord&cfnumber=15-1343.

Camhi, T. (2017, October 9). How Berkeley Became the First City to Ditch Columbus Day for Indigenous Peoples Day. *SF Gate*. www.sfgate.com /bayarea/article/How-Berkeley-became-the-first-city-to-ditch-12265035.php.

Carey, M. (2018, January 24). Australia Day Remains a Culture War Battleground. *SBS*. www.sbs.com.au/nitv/nitv/article/2018/01/23/opinion-australia-day-remains-culture-war-battleground-if-australia-day-falls.

Carr, J. B. and Feiock, R. C. eds. (2016). *City-County Consolidation and Its Alternatives: Reshaping the Local Government Landscape*. New York: Routledge.

Carr Smyth, J. (2018, October 8). No Columbus Day in Columbus. *Associated Press*. https://apnews.com/a944b3d3a2984f48a77b16217de3af6a.

Castle, J. 2019. New Fronts in the Culture Wars? Religion, Partisanship, and Polarization on Religious Liberty and Transgender Rights in the United States. *American Politics Research*, 47(3), 650–679.

Chappell, B. (2018, October 8). Columbus, Ohio, Is Not Observing Columbus Day This Year. *NPR*. www.npr.org/2018/10/08/655640579/columbus-ohio-is-not-observing-columbus-day-this-year.

Chou, M. and Busbridge, R. (2019) Culture Wars, Local Government and the Australia Day Controversy: Insights from Urban Politics Research. *Urban Policy and Research*, 37(3), 367–377.

City of Columbus (2013, November 7). City of Columbus to Honor Veterans Day. www.columbus.gov/Templates/Detail.aspx?id=62695.

City of Columbus (2018, October 5). City of Columbus Open on Columbus Day. www.columbus.gov/Templates/Detail.aspx?id=?147506287.

Clure, F. (2017, August 22). Melbourne's City of Darebin Council Decides to Dump Australia Day Ceremonies. *ABC News*. www.abc.net.au/news/2017-08-21/darebin-council-decision-on-australia-day-ceremonies/8828198.

Cobb, R. W. and Ross, M. H. (1997). *Cultural Strategies of Agenda Denial: Avoidance, Attack, and Redefinition*. Lawrence, KS: University of Kansas Press.

Cochrane, A. (2004). Modernisation, Managerialism and the Culture Wars: Reshaping the Local Welfare State in England. *Local Government Studies*, 30(4), 481–496.

Collier, D., LaPorte, J., and Seawright, J. (2012). Putting Typologies to Work: Concept Formation, Measurement, and Analytical Rigor. *Political Research Quarterly*, 65(1), 217–232.

Columbus City Council. (2019, April 17). To Oppose and Condemn the Enactment of the 133rd General Assembly's Six-week Abortion Ban through Substitute Senate Bill 23. *City of Columbus*, 0129X-2019. https://columbus.legistar.com/LegislationDetail.aspx?ID=3919884&GUID=8A5798FE-0E8B-488A-88A2-9869498DEE8A&Options=&Search=.

Commonwealth of Australia (2019). *Australian Citizenship Ceremonies Code*. https://immi.homeaffairs.gov.au/citizenship-subsite/files/australian-citizenship-ceremonies-code.pdf.

Craw, M. (2006). Overcoming City Limits: Vertical and Horizontal Models of Local Redistributive Policymaking. *Social Sciences Quarterly*, 87(2), 361–379.

Curl, J. (2012, September 28). 20 Years Later – The Origins of Indigenous Peoples Day. *The Berkeley Daily Planet*. www.berkeleydailyplanet.com/issue/2012-09-28/article/40260.

Curl, J. (2016). A Documentary History of the Origin and Development of Indigenous Peoples Day, Berkeley. *Archives of Indigenous Peoples Day*. www.ipdpowwow.org/Archives_3.html.

Dalmat, D. M. (2003). Bringing Economic Justice Closer to Home: The Legal Viability of Local Minimum Wage Laws under Home Rule. *Columbia Journal of Law and Social Problems*, 39(1), 93–147.

Darebin City Council (2017, August 21). Minutes of the Council Meeting. www.darebin.vic.gov.au/-/media/cityofdarebin/Files/YourCouncil/HowCouncilWorks/MeetingAgendasMinutes/CouncilMeetings/2017/21Aug/Minutes-21August2017.ashx?la=en.

Davis, M. (2014). The Culture Wars and Public Policy. In C. Miller and L. Orchard (eds.), *Australian Public Policy: Progressive Ideas in a Neo-Liberal Ascendency* (27–44). Bristol: Policy Press.

Davis, M. (2018). "Culture Is Inseparable from Race": Culture Wars from Pat Buchanan to Milo Yiannopoulos. *M/C Journal: A Journal of Media and Culture*, 21(5). http://journal.media-culture.org.au/index.php/mcjournal/article/view/1484.

DeLeon, R. (1999). San Francisco and Domestic Partners: New Fields of Battle in the Culture War. In E. B. Sharp (ed.), *Culture Wars and Local Politics* (117–136). Lawrence, KS: University of Kansas Press.

DeLeon, R. and Naff, K. C. (2004). Identity Politics and Political Culture: Some Comparative Results from the Social Capital Benchmark Survey. *Urban Affairs Review*, 39(6), 689–719.

Denters, B. and Rose, L. E. (2005), *Comparing Local Governance: Trends and Developments*. New York: Palgrave Macmillan.

Dewhurst, C., Grant, B., and Huuskes, L. (2018). Party Politics and Local Government in Australia: Stability, Change and Implications for Australia's Polity. Paper presented at the 25th World Conference of Political Science, Brisbane, Australia.

Dollery, B. E., Grant, B., and O'Keefe, S. (2008). Local Councils As Place-Shapers: Implications of the Lyons Report for Australian Local Government. *Australian Journal of Political Science*, 43(3), 481–494.

Dollery, B. E., Goode, S., and Grant, B. (2010). Structural Reform of Local Government in Australia: A Sustainable Amalgamation Model for Country Councils. *Space and Polity*, 14(3), 289–304.

Doumar, K. (2018, October 8). Goodbye, Columbus Day. *CityLab*. www.citylab.com/life/2018/10/why-cities-turned-against-columbus-day/572338/.

Dunn, K. M. (2005). Repetitive and Troubling Discourses of Nationalism in the Local Politics of Mosque Development in Sydney, Australia. *Environment and Planning D*, 23(1), 29–50.

Dunn, K. M., Thompson, S., Hanna, B., Murphy, P., and Burnley, I. (2001). Multicultural Policy within Local Government Australia. *Urban Studies*, 38(13), 2477–2494.

Economou, N. (2010). Parties, Participation and Outcomes: The 2008 Victorian Local Government Elections. *Australian Journal of Political Science*, 45(3), 425–436.

Economou, N. and Ghazarian, Z. (2018). Localism, Diversity, and Volatility: The 2016 Australian Federal Election and the "Rise" of Populism. *Australasian Parliamentary Review*, 33(1), 134–155.

Elazar, D. (1966). *American Federalism: A View from the States*. New York: Thomas Y. Crowell.

Feeney, N. (2014, October 13). How Indigenous Peoples Day Came to Be. *Time*. https://time.com/3495071/indigenous-peoples-day/.

Fetner, T. (2008). *How the Religious Right Shaped Lesbian and Gay Activism.* Minneapolis, MN: University of Minnesota Press,

Fiorina, M. P., Abrams, S. J., and Pope, J. C. (2005). *Culture War? The Myth of a Polarized America.* New York: Pearson Longman.

Fischel, W. A. (2005). *The Homevoter Hypothesis: How Home Values Influence Local Government Taxation, School Finance, and Land-Use Policies.* Cambridge, MA: Harvard University Press.

Flinders Council (2013, November 21). Minutes, Ordinary Council Meeting. www .flinders.tas.gov.au/client-assets/images/Council/Downloads/Minutes/ 2013.11.21%20Confirmed%20Minutes%20Ordinary%20Council%20Meeting .pdf.

Flinders Council (2015, March 26). Confirmed Minutes, Ordinary Council Meeting. www.flinders.tas.gov.au/client-assets/images/Council/Downloads/ Minutes/Confirmed%20Minutes%20Ordinary%20Council%20Meeting% 202015.03.26.pdf.

Flinders Council (2016a, May 19). Minutes, Ordinary Council Meeting. www .flinders.tas.gov.au/client-assets/images/Council/Downloads/Minutes/ 2016.05.19%20Confirmed%20Minutes%20Ordinary%20Council% 20Meeting.pdf.

Flinders Council (2016b, July 14). Agenda of the Ordinary Council Meeting. www.flinders.tas.gov.au/client-assets/images/Council/Downloads/Minutes/ 2016.07.14%20Confirmed%20Minutes%20Ordinary%20Council% 20Meeting.pdf.

Flinders Council (2018). Furneaux Islands Festival Policy. www.flinders.tas.gov .au/client-assets/images/Council/Downloads/Policies/No.%201%20Festival% 20Islands%20Furneaux%20Policy.pdf.

Florida, R. (2017, July/August). A Declaration of Urban Independence. *Politico Magazine.* www.politico.com/magazine/story/2017/06/23/richard-florida-cities-independent-donald-trump-215288.

Flynn, M. (2018, October 8). Columbus, Ohio, Once Spent $95 Million to Help Celebrate Columbus Day. Now, It's Canceled. *Washington Post.* www .washingtonpost.com/news/morning-mix/wp/2018/10/08/columbus-ohio-once-spent-95-million-to-celebrate-columbus-day-now-its-canceled/? noredirect=on.

Fonte, J. (2000, December 1). Why There is a Culture War. *Hoover Policy Review.* www.hoover.org/research/why-there-culture-war.

Fraune, C. and Knodt, M. (2018) Sustainable Energy Transformations in an Age of Populism, Post-Truth Politics, and Local Resistance. *Energy Research and Social Science,* 43, 1–7.

George, J. (2009). Introduction: Are the Culture Wars Over? In J. George and K. Huynh (eds.), *The Culture Wars: Australian and American Politics in the 21st Century* (1–15). South Yarra, Melbourne: Palgrave Macmillan.

George, J. and Huynh, K. eds. (2009). *The Culture Wars: Australian and American Politics in the 21st Century.* South Yarra, Melbourne: Palgrave Macmillan.

Georgio, P., Davis, S., and Murphy, A. (2013). Local Government Electoral Review Discussion Paper. State Government of Victoria.

Ghasarian, C. (1996). Cultural Experimentation in Berkeley. *Urban Anthropology and Studies of Cultural Systems and World Economic Development*, 25(1), 41–74.

Gibbins, R. (2001). Local Governance and Federal Political Systems. *International Social Science Journal*, 55(1), 163–170.

Gibbs, E. (2017, November 29). Local Councils Helping Lift the Unemployed. *Eureka Street.* www.eurekastreet.com.au/article/local-councils-helping-lift-the-unemployed.

Gitlin, T. (1995) *The Twilight of Common Dreams: Why America Is Wracked by Culture Wars.* New York: Metropolitan Books.

Goodman, A. (2014, October 13). Seattle Marks Indigenous People's Day amid Calls to End Federal Holiday Celebrating Columbus. *Democracy Now.* www .democracynow.org/2014/10/13/seattle_marks_indigenous_people_s_day.

Grant, B. and Dollery, B. E. (2010). Place-Shaping by Local Governments in the Developing World: Lessons for the Developed World. *International Journal of Public Administration*, 33(5), 251–261.

Grant, B. and Drew, J. (2017). *Local Government in Australia: History, Theory and Public Policy.* Singapore: Springer.

Grumm, J. G. and Murphy, R. D. (1974). Dillion's Rule Reconsidered. *The Annals of the American Academy of Political and Social Science*, 416, 120–132.

Grunwald, M. (2018, November 3). How Everything Became the Culture War. *Politico.* www.politico.eu/article/democrats-republicans-us-immigration-global-warming-education-how-everything-became-the-culture-war/.

Haider-Markel, D. P. and Meier, K. J. (1996). The Politics of Gay and Lesbian Rights: Expanding the Scope of Conflict. *Journal of Politics*, 58(2), 332–349.

Hais, M., Ross, D., and Winograd, M. (2018). *Healing American Democracy: Going Local.* CreateSpace Independent Publishing Platform. www .golocal.us.com/.

Harbur, M.J . (2018) Charlottesville: First Amendment Freedom Intersects Laws Prohibiting Private Militias and Protecting Public Safety. *State and Local Law News*, American Bar Association. www.americanbar.org/groups/

state_local_government/publications/state_local_law_news/2017-18/win
ter/charlottesville-first-amendment-freedom-intersects-laws prohibiting-pri
vate-militias-and protecting-public-safety/.

Hare, C. and Poole, K. T. (2014). The Polarization of Contemporary American
Politics. *Polity*, 46(3), 411–429.

Hartman, A. (2015). *A War for the Soul of America: A History of the Culture
Wars*. Chicago, IL: University of Chicago Press.

Hartman, A. (2018, May). The Culture Wars are Dead: Long Live the Culture
Wars! *The Baffler*, 39. https://thebaffler.com/outbursts/culture-wars-are-dead
-hartman.

Hay, J. (2011). Popular Culture in a Critique of the New Political Reason.
Cultural Studies, 25(4–5), 659–684.

Hicks, W. D, Weissert, C., Swanson, J., and Bulman-Pozen, J. (2018). Home
Rule Be Damned: Exploring Policy Conflicts between the Statehouse and
City Hall. *PS: Political Science & Politics*, 51(1), 26–38.

Hitchmough, S. (2013). "It's Not Your Country Anymore." Contested National
Narratives and the Columbus Day Parade Protests in Denver. *European
Journal of American Culture*, 32(3), 263–283.

Hobart City Council. (2017a, October 18). Agenda: Community, Culture and
Events Committee Meeting. http://hobart.infocouncil.biz/Open/2017/10/
CCE_18102017_AGN_653_AT_WEB.htm.

Hobart City Council. (2017b, October 18). Minutes of the Ordinary Meeting of
Council. http://hobart.infocouncil.biz/Open/2017/10/CCE_18102017_MIN
_653_WEB.htm.

Hobbs, A. (2014, October 14). Citizens Urge Olympia to Recognize Indigenous
People's Day in 2015. *The Olympian*. www.theolympian.com/news/local/
article26083903.html.

Holder, S. (2019, June 3). The Subtle Ways Cities Are Restricting Abortion
Access. *CityLab*. www.citylab.com/equity/2019/06/abortion-access-
provider-city-where-allowed-zoning-roe-wade/590095/.

Holmes, A. (2019, January 14). Prime Minister's Australia Day Call Unlikely to
Force Changes for Northern Tasmanian Councils. *The Examiner*. www
.examiner.com.au/story/5850063/pms-australia-day-call-unlikely-to-force
changes/.

Hopkins, D. J. (2018). *The Increasingly United States: How and Why American
Political Behavior Nationalized*. Chicago, IL: University of Chicago Press.

Hunter, J. D. (1991). *Culture Wars: The Struggle to Define America*. New York:
Basic.

Hunter, J. D. (1994). *Before the Shooting Begins: Searching for Democracy in
America's Culture War*. New York: The Free Press.

Jackman, S. (2017) Populism and Discontent: Comparing the United States and Australia. *Papers on Parliament no. 67*. www.aph.gov.au/About_Parliament/ Senate/Powers_practice_n_procedures/pops/Papers_on_Parliament_67/ Populism_and_Discontent_Comparing_the_United_States_and_Australia.

Jan, E. (2015, October 12). Head to These Cities for Indigenous Peoples' Day. *The Atlantic*. www.theatlantic.com/politics/archive/2015/10/head-to-these-cities-for-indigenous-peoples-day/433083/.

Karp, P. (2019, September 24). Greens Urge Councils to Challenge Federal Rules Ordering Australia Day Citizenship Ceremonies. *The Guardian*. www .theguardian.com/australia-news/2019/sep/24/greens-urge-councils-to-chal lenge-federal-rules-ordering-australia-day-citizenship-ceremonies.

Katz, B. and Nowak, J. (2017). *The New Localism: How Cities Can Thrive in the Age of Populism*. Washington, DC: Brookings Institution Press.

Kelleher Palus, C. (2010). Responsiveness in American Political Governments. *State and Local Government Review*, 42(2), 133–150.

Kelly, P. (2018, January 27). Australia Day: We Must Face the Two Truths about January 26. *The Australian*. www.theaustralian.com.au/news/inquirer/austra lia-day-wemust-face-the-two-truths-about-january-26/newsstory/ 29e7490c91e7911adc6245d8ecb42199.

KEXP. (2018, October 8). Indigenous People's Day Interview with Matt Remle. *KEXP*. www.kexp.org/read/2018/10/8/indigenous-peoples-day-interview-matt-remle-editor-last-real-indians/.

Kincaid, J. (2017). Introduction: The Trump Interlude and the States of American Federalism. *State and Local Government Review*, 49(3), 156–169.

Kingston City Council. (2018, July 23). Minutes of the Ordinary Meeting of Council. www.kingston.vic.gov.au/files/assets/public/governance/minutes-2018/minutes-ordinary-meeting-of-council-23-july-2018.pdf.

Koch, I. (2017). What's in a Vote? Brexit Beyond the Culture Wars. *American Ethnologist*, 44(2), 225–230.

Kwan, E. (2007) Celebrating Australia: A History of Australia Day. https:// ausdayold.siteinprod.com.au/australia-day/history/.

Leonard, D. J. (2012) *After Artest: The NBA and the Assault on Blackness*. New York: State University of New York Press.

Levine Einstein, K. and Kogan, V. (2016). Pushing the City Limits: Policy Responsiveness in Municipal Government. *Urban Affairs Review*, 52(1), 3–32.

Liechty, D. (2013). Columbus Day. In R. Chapman and J. Ciment (eds.), *Culture Wars in America: An Encyclopedia of Issues, Viewpoints, and Voices* (135). London: Routledge.

Lieske, J. (1993). Regional Subcultures of the United States. *Journal of Politics*, 55(4), 888–913.

Lindblom, C. E. (1959). The Science of "Muddling Through." *Public Administration Review*, 19(2), 79–88.

Lineberry, R. L. and Fowler, E. P. (1967). Reformism and Public Policies in American Cities. *American Political Science Review*, 61(3), 701–716.

Liu, A. (2018, September 21). The Limits of City Power in the Age of Trump. *Brookings Institution Blog*. www.brookings.edu/blog/the-avenue/2018/09/ 21/the-limits-of-city-power-in-the-age-of-trump/.

Loc, T. (2017, August 30). L.A. City Council Votes to Replace Columbus Day with Indigenous Peoples Day. *LAist*. https://laist.com/2017/08/30/indigen ous_peoples_day.php.

Los Angeles City Council. (2015, November 13). Motion (e). https://cityclerk .lacity.org/lacityclerkconnect/index.cfm?fa=ccfi.viewrecord&cfnumber=15-1343.

Los Angeles City Council. (2017a, August 30). Motion 13-C. https://cityclerk .lacity.org/lacityclerkconnect/index.cfm?fa=ccfi.viewrecord&cfnumber=15-1343.

Los Angeles City Council. (2017b, August 30). Motion 13-D. https://cityclerk .lacity.org/lacityclerkconnect/index.cfm?fa=ccfi.viewrecord&cfnumber=15-1343.

Los Angeles City Council. (2017c, August 30). Official Action of the Los Angeles City Council (Motion 13-D). https://cityclerk.lacity.org/lacityclerk connect/index.cfm?fa=ccfi.viewrecord&cfnumber=15-1343.

Los Angeles Housing and Community Investment Department (2016, October 25). Indigenous Peoples Day Report. https://cityclerk.lacity.org/laci tyclerkconnect/index.cfm?fa=ccfi.viewrecord&cfnumber=15-1343.

Lyle, J. (2016, October 6). City of Yakima to Replace Columbus Day with Indigenous People's Day. *KIMA TV*. https://kimatv.com/news/local/city-of-yakima-will-no-longer-celebrate-columbus-day.

Mansell, M. (2016, January 25). Let's Change Our National Holiday. *The Mercury*. www.themercury.com.au/news/opinion/talking-point-lets-change-our-nationalholiday/news-story/24e7c2dba85fa943b348f2941d5aa01f.

Markowski, R. (2011). Responsiveness. In B. Badie, D. Berg-Schosser, and L. Morlino (eds.), *International Encyclopedia of Political Science* (2303–2306). Thousand Oaks, CA: Sage.

Marone, J. A. (2014). Political Culture: Consensus, Conflict, and Culture War. In R. Valelly, S. Mettler, and R. Liebermann (eds.) *The Oxford Handbook of American Political Development* (132–147). Oxford: Oxford University Press.

Masanauskas, J. (2017, August 22). Darebin Council Votes to Dump Australia Day, Loses Right to Hold Citizenship Ceremonies. *Herald*

Sun. www.heraldsun.com.au/news/national/darebin-council-votes-to-dump-australia-day/news-story/1ad7c29e9e2d9b681a80a12e506a310f.

Maynor-Lowery, M. (2019, October 14) Why More Places Are Abandoning Columbus Day in Favor of Indigenous Peoples' Day. *Salon*. www.salon.com /2019/10/14/why-more-places-are-abandoning-columbus-day-in-favor-of-indigenous-peoples-day_partner.

McBride, D. (2010). Counterculture. In W. Deverell and G. Hise (eds.), *A Companion to Los Angeles* (327–345). Malden, MA: Wiley Blackwell.

McKnight, D. (2005). *Beyond Right and Left: New Politics and the Culture Wars*. Crows Nest, New South Wales: Allen and Unwin.

McReynolds, D. (2015, November 14). L.A. City Councilman Wants to Establish "Indigenous People's Day." *LAist*. https://laist.com/2015/11/14/ goodbye_columbus.php.

Meier, K. J. (1994). *The Politics of Sin: Drugs, Alcohol and Public Policy*. Armonk, NY: Sharpe.

Melzer, S. (2009). *Gun Crusaders: The NRA's Culture War*. New York: New York University Press.

Mintrom, M. and Norman P. (2009). Policy Entrepreneurship and Policy Change. *Policy Studies Journal*, 37(4), 648–667.

Moffitt, B. (2016) *The Global Rise of Populism: Performance, Political Style, and Representation*. Stanford, CA: Stanford University Press.

Moffitt, B. (2017) Populism in Australia and New Zealand. In C. R. Kaltwasser, P. Taggart, P. O. Espejo, and P. Ostiguy (eds.), *The Oxford Handbook of Populism* (121–139). Oxford: Oxford University Press.

Morgado, D. (2018, February 2). How This US City Replaced "Columbus Day" with "Indigenous People Day." *Culture Trip*. https://theculturetrip.com/ north-america/usa/articles/us-city-replaced-columbus-day-indigenous-people-day/.

Müller, J.-W. (2019). Populism and the People. *London Review of Books*, 41 (10), 35–37. www.lrb.co.uk/the-paper/v41/n10/jan-werner-mueller/popu lism-and-the-people.

Mundstock, D. (1985). Berkeley in the 70s: A History of Progressive Electoral Politics. https://berkeleyinthe70s1.homesteadcloud.com/e-71-73.

Murdock, J. (2018, October 8). What Is Indigenous Peoples' Day? Cities across America Ditch Columbus Day to Recognize New Holiday. *Newsweek*. www .newsweek.com/what-indigenous-people-day-cities-across-america-ditch-columbus-day-recognize-1157792.

Murphy, H. (2019, April 28). Maine Is the Latest State to Replace Columbus Day with Indigenous Peoples' Day. *The New York Times*. www.nytimes.com /2019/04/28/us/columbus-day-indigenous-peoples.html.

Murphy, H. and Ortiz, A. (2019, October 13). Columbus Day or Indigenous Peoples' Day? Depends Where You Are. *The New York Times*. www .nytimes.com/2019/10/13/us/indigenous-peoples-day-columbus-day.html.

Nagle, M. (2014, November 6). History Is Made on Indigenous Peoples' Day. *LRInspire*. https://lrinspire.com/2014/11/06/history-is-made-on-indigenous-peoples-day-by-matt-nagle/.

New York Times. (1992, January 12). In Berkeley, Day for Columbus Is Renamed. *The New York Times*. www.nytimes.com/1992/01/12/us/in-berkeley-day-for-columbus-is-renamed.html.

Norris, P. and Inglehart, R. (2019). *Cultural Backlash: Trump, Brexit, and Authoritarian Populism*. Cambridge: Cambridge University Press.

Norwood, J. (2016, November 23). Standing in Solidarity. *Our Weekly*. http:// ourweekly.com/news/2016/nov/23/standing-solidarity/.

O'Hanlon, S. and Sharpe, S. (2009). Becoming Post-Industrial: Victoria Street Fitzroy, c. 1970 to Now. *Urban Policy and Research*, 27(3), 289–300.

Oliver, J. E. (2012). *Local Elections and the Politics of Small-Scale Democracy*. Princeton,NJ: Princeton University Press.

Olsen, H. (2019, October 15). Getting Rid of Columbus Day Entirely Is a Sad Development. *The Washington Post*. www.washingtonpost.com/opinions/ 2019/10/14/we-could-abolish-columbus-day-we-shouldnt/?stream=to p&utm_campaign=newsletter_axiospm&utm_medium=email&utm_sour ce=newsletter.

Percy, K. (2017, August 17). Australia Day: Local Cheer Despite PM's Warning over Yarra Ending References to National Holiday. *ABC News*. www .abc.net.au/news/2017-08-16/australia-day-city-of-yarra-reacts/8813364.

Perez, C. (2018, October 8). Columbus, Ohio Cancels Columbus Day. *New York Post*. https://nypost.com/2018/10/08/columbus-ohio-cancels-columbus -day/.

Peterson, P. E. (1981). *City Limits*. Chicago, IL: University of Chicago Press.

Phillips, J. (2016, October 10). The War against Columbus Day. *The Washington Post*. www.washingtonpost.com/news/post-nation/wp/2016/10/ 10/the-war-against-columbus-day/.

Polignano, M. J. (2010). *Taking Our Own Side*. San Francisco, CA: Counter-Currents.

Pruijt, H. (2013). Culture Wars, Revanchism, Moral Panics and the Creative City. A Reconstruction of a Decline of Tolerant Public Policy: The Case of Dutch Anti-squatting Legislation. *Urban Studies*, 50(6), 1114–1129.

Putnam, R. D. and Campbell, D. E. (2010). *American Grace: How Religion Divides and Unites Us*. New York: Simon and Schuster.

Rao, S. (2017, August 31). Los Angeles Is Largest US City to Replace Columbus Day with Indigenous Peoples' Day. *Colorlines*. www.colorlines .com/articles/los-angeles-largest-us-city-replace-columbus-day-indigenous-peoples-day.

Reese, A. and Rosenfeld, R. A. (2012). *Comparative Civic Culture: The Role of Local Culture in Urban Policy-Making*. Farnham, UK: Ashgate.

Remle, M. (2014, October 14). Community Unites to Start Indigenous Peoples' Day. *Indianz.com*. www.indianz.com/News/2014/10/14/matt-remle-community-unites-to.asp.

Remle, M. (2018, August 2). Organizing for Change. *Last Real Indians*. https:// lastrealindians.com/news/2018/8/2/aug-2-2018-organizing-for-change-by-matt-remle.

Remle, M. (2019, March 27). Kshama Solidarity. *Facebook*. www .facebook.com/VoteSawant/videos/167179704166149/.

Rennie, S. (2019, January 15). Darebin Mayor: We Are Not Anti-Australia Day, Just Not on January 26. *The Age*. www.theage.com.au/national/victoria/dar ebin-mayor-we-are-not-anti-australia-day-just-not-on-january-26-20190115-p50rgk.html.

Review Partners (2018, January). *Australia Day 2018: A Turning Point for Our National Identity?* http://docs.wixstatic.com/ugd/1316a9_751b120a342e475ab0 b938243ad38fdf.pdf.

Rosdil, D. (1991). The Context of Radical Populism in US Cities: A Comparative Analysis. *Journal of Urban Affairs*, 13(1), 77–96.

Rosdil, D. (2010). Testing Cultural and Economic Explanations for Local Development Policies: The Competing Claims of Security, Distress, and Nontraditional Subcultures. *Journal of Urban Affairs*, 32(1), 105–130.

Rosdil, D. (2011). Civic Culture, Sub-cultures, Non-traditionalism and Progressive Policy: Using Value Change to Explain New US Development Strategies in the 21st Century. *Urban Studies*, 48(16), 3467–3486.

Rosenberg, G. (2019, April 16). Columbus Council Votes to Condemn Six-Week Abortion Ban. *WOSU Radio*. https://radio.wosu.org/post/columbus-council-votes-condemn-six-week-abortion-ban#stream/0.

Rosenthal, C. S. (2005). Local Politics: A Different Front in the Culture War? *The Forum*, 3(2). www.degruyter.com/view/journals/for/3/2/article-00001022021540888841080.xml?language=en.

Rupar, A. (2019, August 6). Trump Is Visiting El Paso and Dayton. Some Local Officials Aren't Happy. *Vox*. www.vox.com/2019/8/6/20757086/trump-trip-el-paso-dayton-mass-shooting-sites-controversy-explained.

Russell, J. D. and Bostrom, A. (2016, January). Federalism, Dillion Rule and Home Rule. *White Paper: A Publication of the American City County*

Exchange. www.alec.org/app/uploads/2016/01/2016-ACCE-White-Paper-Dillon-House-Rule-Final.pdf.

Ryan, R., Hastings, C., Woods, R., Lawrie, A., and Grant, B. (2015). Why Local Government Matters: Summary Report 2015. Australian Centre of Excellence for Local Government, University of Technology Sydney.

Sabatier, P. A. (1988). An Advocacy Coalition Framework of Policy Change and the Role of Policy-Oriented Therein. *Policy Sciences*, 21(2), 129–168.

Salisbury, R. (1969). An Exchange Theory of Interest Groups. *Midwest Journal of Political Science*, 13(February), 1–32.

Sassen, S. (2001). *The Global City: New York, London, Tokyo*. Princeton, NJ: Princeton University Press.

Schattschneider, E. E. (1960). *The Semi-Sovereign People: A Realist View of Democracy in America*. New York: Holt, Reinhart and Winston.

Schleicher, D. (2007). Why Is There No Partisan Competition in City Council Elections? The Role of Election Law. *Journal of Law and Politics*, 23(4), 419–473.

Schleicher, D. (2017). Federalism and State Democracy. *Texas Law Review*, 95, 763–820.

Schmidt, S. (2017, August 31). In Los Angeles, Columbus Day Is Toppled Like a Confederate Statue. *The Washington Post*. www.washingtonpost.com/news/morning-mix/wp/2017/08/31/in-los-angeles-columbus-day-is-toppled-like-a-confederate-statute/.

Schneider, M. and Teske, P. (1992). Toward a Theory of Political Entrepreneur: Evidence from Local Government. *American Political Science Review*, 86(3), 737–747.

Schneider, M. and Teske, P. (1993). The Progrowth Entrepreneur in Local Government. *Urban Affairs Review*, 29(2), 316–327.

Schumaker, P. (1999). Moral Principles of Local Officials and the Resolution of Culture War Issues. In E. B. Sharp (ed.), *Culture Wars and Local Politics* (193–219). Lawrence, KS: University of Kansas Press.

Seattle City Council. (2014, October 6). Resolution 31538: A Resolution Relating to Indigenous Peoples' Day. http://clerk.seattle.gov/search/results?d=RESF&s1=31538.resn.&Sect6=HITOFF&l=20&p=1&u=/~public/resn1.htm&r=1&f=G.

Sehorn, G. F. (2019). Culture War Skirmishes in Public Schools: The Experience of Evangelical Christian Administrators. *Religion & Education*, 46(2), 252–270.

Sharp, E. B. (1996). Culture Wars and City Politics: Local Government's Role in Social Conflict. *Urban Affairs Review*, 31(6), 738–758.

Sharp, E. B. (1997). A Comparative Anatomy of Urban Social Conflict. *Political Research Quarterly*, 50(2), 261–280.

Sharp, E. B. ed. (1999a). *Culture Wars and Local Politics*. Lawrence, KS: University of Kansas Press.

Sharp, E. B. (1999b). Introduction. In E. B. Sharp (ed.), *Culture Wars and Local Politics* (1–20). Lawrence, KS: University of Kansas Press.

Sharp, E. B. (1999c). Conclusion. In E. B. Sharp (ed.), *Culture Wars and Local Politics* (220–240). Lawrence, KS: University of Kansas Press.

Sharp, E. B. (2002). Culture, Institutions, and Urban Officials' Response to Morality Issues. *Political Research Quarterly*, 55(4), 861–883.

Sharp, E. B. (2003). Local Government and the Politics of Decency. *Social Science Quarterly*, 84(2), 262–277.

Sharp, E. B. (2005). *Morality Politics in American Cities*. Lawrence, KS: University of Kansas Press.

Sharp, E. B. (2007). Revitalizing Urban Research: Can Cultural Explanation Bring Us Back from the Periphery? *Urban Affairs Review*, 43(1), 55–75.

Sharp, E. B. and Brown, M. (2012) Cultural Conflicts, Religion and Urban Politics. In P. John, K. Mossberger, and S. E. Clarke (eds.), *The Oxford Handbook of Urban Politics* (394–414). Oxford: Oxford University Press.

Shine, R. (2018, January 14). Australia Day: Five Years Ago, Flinders Island Community Quietly Axed Celebrations. *ABC News*. www.abc.net.au/news/2018-01-14/australia-day-flinders-islandfestivities/9326976.

Shipan, C. R. and Volden, C. (2006). Bottom-up Federalism: The Spread of Antismoking Laws from U.S. Cities to States. *American Journal of Political Science*, 50(4), 825–843.

Shipan, C. R. and Volden, C. (2008). The Mechanisms of Policy Diffusion. *American Journal of Political Science*, 52(4), 840–857.

Slezak, M. (2017, July 19). Australian Local Councils Lead the Way in Tackling Climate Change As Federal Policy Stalls. *The Guardian*. www.theguardian.com/australia-news/2017/jul/19/australian-local-councils-lead-the-way-in-tackling-climate-change-as-federal-policy-stalls.

Smith, J. (2017) Local Responses to Right-Wing Populism: Building Human Rights Cities. *Studies in Social Justice*, 11(2), 347–368.

Somerville, M. (2015). *Bird on an Ethics Wire: Battles about Values in the Culture Wars*. Quebec: McGill-Queen's University Press.

Somin, I. (2013). *Democracy and Political Ignorance*. Palo Alto, CA: Stanford University Press.

Somin, I. (2019a, July 12). How Liberals Learned to Love Federalism. *The Washington Post*. www.washingtonpost.com/outlook/how-liberals-learned-

to-love-federalism/2019/07/12/babd9f52-8c5f-11e9-b162-8f6f41ec3c04_
story.html.

Somin, I. (2019b). Making Federalism Great Again: How the Trump
Administration's Attack on Sanctuary Cities Unintentionally Strengthened
Judicial Protection for State Autonomy. *Texas Law Review*, 97, 1247–1294.

Stein, M. A. (1986, November 3). Progressives in Berkeley Challenged by
Tradition. *Los Angeles Times*. https://articles.latimes.com/1986-11-03/
news/mn-14900_1_runoff-election.

Stoker, G. (2011). Was Local Governance Such a Good Idea? A Global
Comparative Perspective. *Public Administration*, 89(1), 15–31.

Stone, A. (2017, August 18). Yarra Mayor: This Is Why We Unrecognised
Australia Day. *The Sydney Morning Herald*. www.smh.com.au/opinion/
yarra-mayor-this-is-why-we-unrecognisedaustralia-day-20170818-gxz7g3
.html.

Stone, D. A. (2012). *Policy Paradox: The Art of Political Decision Making*.
New York: W. W. Norton & Co.

Tang, A. (2017, October 8). Berkeley Celebrates 25 Years of Indigenous
Peoples' Day. *The Daily Californian*. www.dailycal.org/2017/10/08/berke
ley-community-reflects-cultural-impact-indigenous-peoples-day/.

Tarrow, S. (1994). *Power in Movement: Collective Action, Social Movements
and Politics*. Cambridge: Cambridge University Press.

Tatalovich, R. and Daynes, B. W. eds. (1988). *Social Regulatory Policy:
Moral Controversies in American Politics*. Boulder, CO: Westview
Press.

Taylor, J. K., Tadlock, B., Poggione, S., and DiSarro, B. (2014). Transgender
Inclusive Ordinances in the Cities: Form of Government, Local Politics, and
Vertical Influences. In J. K. Taylor and D. P. Haider-Markel (eds.),
*Transgender Rights and Politics: Groups, Issue Framing, and Policy
Adoption* (135–154). Ann Arbor, MI: University of Michigan Press.

Taylor, J. K., Haider-Markel, D. P., and Lewis, D. C. (2018a). Tensions over
Gay and Transgender Rights between Localities and States. *PS: Political
Science & Politics*, 51(1), 35–37.

Taylor, J. K., Haider-Markel, D. P., and Lewis, D. C. (2018b). *The
Remarkable Rise of Transgender Rights*. Ann Arbor, MI: University of
Michigan Press.

Thomas-Wilson, S. (2017, October 24). Hobart to Officially Support Change of
Australia Day Date. *The Mercury*. www.themercury.com.au/news/politics/
hobart-to-officially-support-change-of-australia-day-date/news-story
/b97905dc2699e666238f7e29945ae8d9.

Thomson, I. T. (2010). *Culture Wars and Enduring American Dilemmas*. Ann Arbor, MI: University of Michigan Press.

Thornton, P. (2017, October 14). Opinion: Not a Fan of Columbus Day or Indigenous Peoples Day? Here Are Some Alternatives. *Los Angeles Times*. www.latimes.com/opinion/readersreact/la-ol-le-columbus-day-indigenous-peoples-20171014-story.html.

Tiffen, R. (2011). We, the Populists. *Griffith Review Edition: Ways of Seeing*, 31. https://griffithreview.com/articles/we-the-populists/.

TIME Magazine. (1992, January 27). Political Correctness: There Go the Coat Sales. *TIME Magazine*. http://content.time.com/time/subscriber/article/0,33009,974727,00.html.

Ting, I. (2017, February 19). Melbourne's Political Geography Revealed in Seven Maps. *The Age*. www.theage.com.au/national/victoria/melbournes-political-geography-revealed-in-seven-maps-20170217-gufqtq.html.

Tobias, J. (2017, March 24). These Cities Are Pulling Billions from the Banks That Support the Dakota Access Pipeline. *Occupy.com*. www.occupy.com/article/these-cities-are-pulling-billions-banks-support-dakota-access-pipe line?qt-article_tabs=1#sthash.lsQfVBzZ.dpbs.

Wahlquist, C. (2017, August 16). Yarra Council Stripped of Citizenship Ceremony Powers after Australia Day Changes. *The Guardian*. www.theguar dian.com/australia-news/2017/aug/16/yarra-council-stripped-of-citizenship-ceremony-powers-after-australia-day-changes.

Whitson, R. (2017, June 20). Australia Day: Local Government Backs Push for National Debate on Date Change. *ABC*. www.abc.net.au/news/2017-06-20/national-support-of-australia-day-date-change/8636134.

Wilkins, K. (2018, January 21). Furneaux Islands Festival Celebrates Art, Music and Culture. *The Examiner*. www.examiner.com.au/story/5179317/furneaux-islands-festival-celebrates-art-music-and-culture/.

Wills, J. (2015) Populism, Localism and the Geography of Democracy. *Geoforum*, 62, 188–189.

Writ, C .L. (1989). Dillion's Rule. *Virginia Town and City*, 24(8). http://578125292684560794.weebly.com/uploads/3/7/7/1/37714259/dillon_ru le_article.pdf.

Yakima City Council. (2016a, October 4). Yakima City Council Minutes. https://yakima.novusagenda.com/agendapublic/DisplayAgendaPDF.ashx? MinutesMeetingID=507.

Yakima City Council. (2016b, October 13). Resolution Changing the Name of Columbus Day to Indigenous Peoples' Day in the City of Yakima. https://yakima.novusagenda.com/agendapublic/CoverSheet.aspx?ItemID=4469&Me etingID=567.

Yakima City Council. (2016c, October 18). Yakima City Council Minutes. https://yakima.novusagenda.com/agendapublic/DisplayAgendaPDF.ashx? MinutesMeetingID=511.

Yakima City Council. (2016d, November 1). Yakima City Council Minutes. https://yakima.novusagenda.com/agendapublic/DisplayAgendaPDF.ashx? MinutesMeetingID=513.

Yarra City Council (2015) Aboriginal Partnerships Plan 2015–2018. www .yarracity.vic.gov.au/the-area/aboriginal-yarra.

Yarra City Council (2017a, August 15). Ordinary Meeting of Council Agenda. www.yarracity.vic.gov.au/-/media/files/council-and-committee-meetings/coun cil-meetings/2017-council-meetings/20170815-ordinary-council-agenda.pdf? la=en&hash=26D7013AD4B59FFA995F59FC636BC5DDF6E7347D.

Yarra City Council (2017b, August 15). Yarra City Council Decision on January 26. www.yarracity.vic.gov.au/news/2017/08/15/yarra-city-council-decision-on-january-26.

Yarra City Council (2017c, August 21). Learn More about Changes to 26 January. www.yarracity.vic.gov.au/news/2017/08/21/learn-more-about-changes-to-26-january.

Zahniser, D. (2017). L.A. City Council Replaces Columbus Day with Indigenous Peoples Day on City Calendar. *Los Angeles Times.* www.latimes.com/local/ lanow/la-me-ln-indigenous-peoples-day-20170829-story.html.

Zavodnyik, P. (2011). *The Rise of the Federal Colossus: The Growth of Federal Power from Lincoln to F.D.R.* Santa Barbara, CA: Praeger.

Zimmerman, J. F. (2008). *Contemporary American Federalism: The Growth of National Power.* Albany, NY: State University of New York Press.

Acknowledgments

First, we would like to thank the series editors, Rob Christensen and Andy Whitford, for working with us in developing and refining this Element. This work has been made better by their suggestions. Second, we would like to acknowledge the thoughtful feedback of our reviewer, who helped us to clarify and better justify the analysis within these pages. Third, we would like to thank Noah Riseman and Haydn Aarons. It was Noah who suggested Columbus Day as a possible comparative case, and Haydn was instrumental in helping us get past a methodological roadblock. Fourth, we thank the local councillors and mayors who helped inform this research. We greatly appreciate their insights.

Finally, we would like to dedicate this Element to our mums – Linda and Helen.

Cambridge Elements ≡

Public and Nonprofit Administration

Andrew Whitford
University of Georgia
Andrew Whitford is Alexander M. Crenshaw Professor of Public Policy in the School
of Public and International Affairs at the University of Georgia. His research centers
on strategy and innovation in public policy and organization studies.

Robert Christensen
Brigham Young University
Robert Christensen is professor and George Romney Research Fellow
in the Marriott School at Brigham Young University. His research focuses
on prosocial and antisocial behaviors and attitudes in public
and nonprofit organizations.

About the Series

The foundation of this series are cutting-edge contributions on emerging topics
and definitive reviews of keystone topics in public and nonprofit administration,
especially those that lack longer treatment in textbook or other formats.
Among keystone topics of interest for scholars and practitioners of public
and nonprofit administration, it covers public management, public budgeting
and finance, nonprofit studies, and the interstitial space between the public and
nonprofit sectors, along with theoretical and methodological contributions,
including quantitative, qualitative and mixed-methods pieces.

The Public Management Research Association

The Public Management Research Association improves public governance
by advancing research on public organizations, strengthening links among
interdisciplinary scholars, and furthering professional and academic opportunities
in public management.

Cambridge Elements $\equiv$

Public and Nonprofit Administration

Elements in the Series

Motivating Public Employees
Marc Esteve and Christian Schuster

Organizational Obliviousness: Entrenched Resistance to Gender Integration in the Military
Alesha Doan and Shannon Portillo

Partnerships that Last: Identifying the Keys to Resilient Collaboration
Heather Getha-Taylor

Behavioral Public Performance: How People Make Sense of Government Metrics
Oliver James, Donald P. Moynihan, Asmus Leth Olsen and Gregg G. Van Ryzin

Redefining Development: Resolving Complex Challenges in Developing Countries
Jessica Kritz

Gender, Risk and Leadership: The Glass Cliff in Public Service Careers
Leisha DeHart-Davis, Deneen Hatmaker, Kim Nelson, Sanjay K. Pandey, Sheela Pandey and Amy Smith

Institutional Memory as Storytelling: How Networked Government Remembers
Jack Corbett, Dennis Christian Grube, Heather Caroline Lovell and Rodney James Scott

How Local Governments Govern Culture War Conflicts
Mark Chou and Rachel Busbridge

A full series listing is available at: www.cambridge.org/EPNP

Printed in the United States
By Bookmasters